SINGLE

DATING

FRIENDSHIPS

& ROMANCE

QUESTIONS FOR ALL OF YOUR ANSWERS

A 40-DAY DEVOTIONAL
BY HEATHER FLIES & TONY MYLES

PUBLISHED BY YM360

HOW TO USE THIS BOOK

There are some things in this book you're interested in now more than others. Still, don't skip around…everything builds on everything else, and you'll get way more out of it by reading it all from start to finish. It'll all be incredibly valuable to you one day, be it for your own journey or to help a friend who's working through that topic.

Notice that each chapter begins and ends with a question, too. This is so that you trade in whatever "answers" you've been living with for something healthier. For example, maybe you've concluded, "I'm ready to date." If so, check out chapter one: "Can You Be Trusted With A Pen?" If you're thinking, "Everyone should just trust me," wait until you read "How Full Is Your Cereal Bowl?" Every chapter will challenge some of your answers.

Here are a few other things you need to know to make this book meaningful for you.

Make This Book A Priority

Pretty much every Christ-follower, no matter how old they may or may not be, struggles to spend meaningful time with God every day. If you're going to learn from this book and be impacted by it, you have to decide that it's important to you. The truth is that you really can learn and grow from reading this book. But it has to matter. So, commit to spending at least 5-10 minutes each day with this book.

Have Your Bible Open

Resist the urge to ignore the spots where this book will tell you to read a passage of Scripture. This book is only a guide for THE Book (your Bible). The spiritual growth and the close relationship with God that you want only happens by reading and doing what's in the Bible. So have your Bible or a Bible app open and a pen or pencil available as you go through this book. Even if the passage is listed in the chapter, read it in your own Bible so you can perhaps consider another translation or paraphrase, and take notes on it.

The Book Is Designed To Help You Stick With It

This devotional study through singleness, dating, friendships, and romance was designed to be completed in 40 days. You can either split it up into 8 five-day weeks and skip the weekends or go through it in 40 straight days. Whichever way you decide to go, you'll read a question, some Scripture, and a short devotional every day. After that, each day will provide you with an interactive activity for honest reflection and prompts to guide you in responding to what you learn. There's plenty of space there and throughout each devotional to journal your thoughts, jot down things from that day's study or Scriptures that stuck out to you, and note any follow-up questions you might have. Don't just think about your answer – write it out.

What If I Miss A Day of Reading? Or Three?

Don't give up! Take this at your own pace! Even better, read it with friends so you can help each other get more out of it. The goal is your spiritual growth and for you to grow closer to God. If you miss a day or two . . . or four . . . don't throw in the towel. Instead, pick this book back up and start where you left off. You can do this!

Table of
CONTENTS

Nice To Meet You!

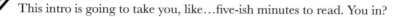

This intro is going to take you, like…five-ish minutes to read. You in?

First…can we let you in on a little secret?

We're not complete experts on what's in this book.

Hang out with us, though, because we have been teachable students of all of this for a long time. We still are.

No one knows the exact right "formula" for what it means to be your age and be single, or what to do when you like someone, or if dating is right/wrong for you, or if you should spend gazillions on fancy clothes so you can go to the next big dance, or if you should make your date homemade lasagna, or…you get the idea.

There's a lot of advice floating around on all of this, though, right? People of all ages all around you, online and in celebrity culture, are probably telling you to do "whatever makes you feel happy." In response, other well-meaning people are likewise telling you to *not* do what all those first people are telling you to do.

We've seen this play out for years. For a while (in something called "the nineties"), it seemed like the ultimate Christian love life thing to do was to sign a pledge saying you wouldn't have sex until you were married. That is a fantastic commitment because it does save something uniquely special for your future spouse (assuming you get married one day, which not everyone does).

Only…what about all the other stuff?

Like, is it okay to hold hands with…or hug…or cuddle with…or pucker up for…a special guy or girl who makes your heartbeat sound like a tough car driving around with the bass turned up?

Or, when could (or should) you use the "L-word" (no, not lasagna) to describe your feelings for someone (or lasagna)?

And is it healthy or not to secretly wonder about marriage when you're on your first date? What if they want to start publicly talking about baby names on your first date? (Psst... run, just run...unless they're going into the baby-naming business one day professionally. If so, you can just sort of jog away as you politely clap about their weird job choice.) Can we let you in on another little secret?

We're not going to just answer these questions for you. That would be just us being another voice in your life telling you "what" to do without helping you know the "why."

Yes, we'll talk all about some of the AMAZING answers that God can share with you throughout the Bible on all of these topics. Those answers are there, often contained in the details of flawed people who sometimes got it all right and other times got it all wrong. It's just that before we show you those answers, we're going to help you understand the questions...not just the ones you're asking, but the questions under those questions that are even better to ask.

We're Heather and Tony, by the way. Nice to meet you! You pronounce our last names, Flies and Myles, as "Fleece" and "Miles" (which sounds like a buddy-cop action movie, doesn't it?).

We've worked with middle school, high school, and college students over the years (and all their parents, by the way) and have personally seen some healthy and tragic stories when people we cared about made decisions one way or another about their singleness, relationships, affection, temptations, and more.

We've also spent oodles of time working on practical and timely teaching to help teenagers and young adults tackle all of this. Some of our amazingly smart friends we enjoy learning from will let you in on their wisdom throughout this book, too.

The most important of those friends, by the way, is God Himself. Seriously. We're going to bring you right up to connecting with Him through every devotional because one day, you'll put this book down (after you've read it hundreds of times and bought thousands of copies for your friends so you can all go through it together – we thank you in advance for that, by the way).

God, though? He's with you in every moment of every day of every week of every month of every year. He loves you, has breathtaking purpose for you, fights for your best, and has taken the time to write so much down for you...because you don't have to guess at life, singleness, and love when you surrender to God and let Him personally lead you through it.

This book will work best when you write in it. Circle stuff that stands out to you. Scribble in answers in the spaces we've created for you to figure some things out. Show ideas that stand out to you to people around you so they can start asking better questions, too. Bottom line: don't just read everything. Wrestle with it.

That's how you get stronger…by wrestling with stuff. It's also how you can become a professional wrestler, probably. If you do, you can even pick out a super tough name for yourself, like…"Lasagna."

We're on this journey with you!

Together,

Heather! Elias
Tony Myles

CAN YOU BE TRUSTED WITH A PEN?

You may have a pen in your fingers right now. If not, maybe you recently did.
Are you the type of person who treats a pen for what it was meant for? You know, like…
you write stuff with it, and then you put it down, and then you pick it up when it makes
sense to use it again, and so on?

Or are you more likely to (maybe without thinking about it) clickity-click-click it, or pick
around at it, or stick it in your mouth, or bite it while you think…and then you look down
and see your nasty drool or teeth marks on it, and think, "Ugh! This is gross. I need a new
pen that doesn't look like it was tossed into a ball pit of toddlers at Chuck-E-Cheese." But
then you sort of just start gnawing and abusing that next pen.

Oh, and have you ever had a pen randomly fall apart or maybe even explode on you?
And you think, "Well, this is horrible. What fool made this pen so ready to just break
down on me?" Maybe it was actually you, or it may have been someone else who damaged it, and you were just the next person to grab it.

The point is, do you think you can be trusted with a pen?

☑ Yes ☐ No ☐ What's a pen? Is that an app on my phone?

Why? (Seriously, answer this. Write it out, you know, with a pen or something.)

I don't chew or click on it a lot.

And then, what do you sense God wants you to notice in this verse?

*The fear of the Lord is the beginning of knowledge; fools despise wisdom
and instruction. (Proverbs 1:7)*

The foundation of my realationship with
God should be built on an healthy fear of
God.

With that in mind…

Do you think you can be trusted with being single?

Do you think you can be trusted with a relationship?

Do you think you can be trusted with being alone with someone you're incredibly attracted to?

"Clickity-click-click."

Or, are you the type of person who treats singleness, relationships, and being alone with someone you're incredibly attracted to for what each of these is meant for?

We just read that the fear of the Lord (meaning to live in awe, respect, and honor of Him in all His great glory, power, purity, holiness, majesty, and so on) is the beginning of knowledge. Your Bible may say "wisdom" instead of "knowledge."

Notice that it doesn't say that knowledge/wisdom is found in fearing the worst but still embracing what you think is best. Like, you get more out of a pen, not when you do everything you can with it right up to the point that it breaks, but when you are teachable and humble about what the pen is designed for.

That may not be the kind of advice you're being given by others, though, about dating, flirting, exploring, and more. Your friends may just be trying to cheer you on when they tell you to "go for it" with some guy or girl who's into you…and they think it's just fine to "clickity-click-click" as long as you can, but then…of course…the whole thing just falls apart, and maybe even breaks.

Be aware, though, that simply being moral isn't the answer either. Lots of well-meaning Christians have made pledges, created challenging routines, worn rings/bracelets, and done more to nudge themselves forward spiritually. Such things can be valuable as secondary things, but they can't be your primary focus because you're utterly incapable of being righteous in your own strength. Even an accountability group where you share your journey with others will only go so far if its theme is, "What's the worst sin you committed this week, and why did you commit it?"

> The reason we mess things up, whether it's our singleness or a relationship, is we're not accustomed to waiting. We get bored, so to speak, and click the pen. We end up doing things that aren't good for us, or we do them out of step with God. When you don't wait for something that's good, problems arise. In fact, you might obtain that thing and realize it's actually not good for you or that you weren't ready for it… but if you had waited, you could have seen that and avoided the trouble to begin with.
> - Adam, 23

The purpose of a pen, and the purpose of your life, is to be placed in the hands of the Author. You can try to fight the heat of lust with cold showers or just white-knuckling through it, or you can embrace the warmth of God's presence and the refreshing words He speaks into you through a relationship with Him. He doesn't just invite you to live according to His wisdom and His knowledge but through His Holy Spirit inside of you.

Ask God what He'd like you to be open to when it comes to singleness and relationships.

Write out a prayer about it right here…it doesn't have to be long, but it does have to come from a genuine place inside of you.

As you do, maybe let that pen you're writing with be a symbol of your life in His hands. Share your heart and ask Him some questions so He can share His heart with you. Be open.

What does God want to trust you with?

WHY NOT DEFINE IT?

That's a great question, isn't it?

Imagine a world where everything and everyone had pop-up labels you could read simply by looking at the object or person. Sure, it might feel weird…but think about how helpful that could be!

You'd look at a random dog, and the pop-up would say, "Friendly to pet!" or "About to puke! Run!"

You'd see a plate of fries at home, and the pop-up would tell you, "Go ahead and sneak one," or "If you touch this, your brother will squirt ketchup on your head."

You'd look at a potential friend or date, and the pop-up would reveal, "This person loves God and will absolutely add to your life," or "This person is creepy. Smile, but quickly turn around and walk away."

What if you were the only person in the world who had this ability?

What if you were the only person in the world who *didn't* have this ability?

Ooooh…did that just unlock a fear? Maybe we avoid defining things so others won't define us. We might be hesitant to say someone's a "best friend" if it means we can't equally hang out with other friends. Maybe we avoid saying, "This is my boyfriend/girlfriend" because of the expectations that hints at. Saying "I'm single" could imply failure in the dating world, and so we sidestep that topic, too.

That's where phrases like "situationship" sprouted. This refers to when a guy and girl regularly hang out and enjoy each other, but neither wants to call it dating. They want the benefits without the risk or commitment. Why does this concept even exist? Who invented it? Why?

Language matters. The source of the language matters more, though.

> Labels can be a good thing to help define limits, but don't rush into placing a label on everything. Take time to pray about not only romantic or potential romantic relationships, but family and friendships as well. This is when real relational growth and maturity begins.
> - Elyse, 20

In our imaginary pop-up world, something we'd have to eventually ask is who's sup̄ ing the information for the pop-ups? What if it was a random kid? What if it was an woman? What if it was your 3rd-grade P.E. teacher? What if it was you? What if it v God? Our music, movies, TV shows, reels, and more all try to put a label on what they are. Who's behind those pop-ups? Should they be?

Why not define who gets to define it? Isn't that an even better question? And how does it all relate to singleness, dating, friendship, and romance? Consider this:

In the beginning, God created the heavens and the earth. (Genesis 1:1)

God is the Creator of everything. It makes sense that He would be the One who defines what's what, right? If so, how do you feel about God having the final say on everything? Write about that. Define it.

Then the Lord God formed the man of dust from the ground and breathed into his nostrils the breath of life, and the man became a living creature... the Lord God took the man and put him in the Garden of Eden to work it and keep it. (Genesis 2:7, 15)

The first human was alone with God AND had a purpose. God later said that human relationships did matter, but that doesn't cancel out what's here: your relationship status with others doesn't determine your value…your relationship status with God does. What will you personally claim about this? Define it.

Then the Lord God said, "It is not good that the man should be alone; I will make him a helper fit for him." Now out of the ground the Lord God had formed every beast of the field and every bird of the heavens and brought them to the man to see what he would call them. And whatever the man called every living creature, that was its name. (Genesis 2:18-19)

This seems odd, doesn't it? God says out loud that it's not good for Adam to be alone, but He doesn't immediately make Eve. Why not? Why did He want Adam to observe the animals and work his job first? If you had to guess, what would be your guess? Define it.

So the Lord God caused a deep sleep to fall upon the man, and while he slept took one of his ribs and closed up its place with flesh. And the rib that the Lord God had taken from the man He made into a woman and brought her to the man. (Genesis 2:21-22)

God could have created Eve with Adam awake and watching, and yet He didn't. Instead, He had a private moment with Eve before bringing her to him. Why might this have mattered to God? What does this mean in your life? Define it.

Then the man said, "This at last is bone of my bones and flesh of my flesh; she shall be called Woman, because she was taken out of Man." Therefore a man shall leave his father and his mother and hold fast to his wife, and they shall become one flesh. And the man and his wife were both naked and were not ashamed. (Genesis 2:23-25)

Adam gets poetic after seeing Eve and realizing she's his wife. What do you think about this? Define it.

The great thing about doing this type of exercise is that now you can more intelligently define singleness, dating, friendship, and romance.

- What if being single means something is right...not wrong?

- What if the purpose of dating is to add to the lives of others?

- What if friendship is how God spreads kindness?

- What if romance is a spiritual thing?

Once you figure that out, keep it going. Ask God more questions, like what counts as a date? Is that fun person you text for hours every day your boyfriend/girlfriend? What does it mean to be a better friend? Sure, it might feel weird...but try to understand how helpful that could be.

What if you didn't have to fear labels anymore but discovered tremendous freedom in defining everything in life from God's perspective? Seriously, write your answer to that question below.

WHAT IF "THE ONE" ISN'T THE ONE YOU'RE THINKING OF?

Most teenagers fall into two groups—those who love math and those who have struggled since the multiplication table was introduced in 2nd grade. Whether you revel in taking college-level math courses or can't wait until you meet the minimum math requirement, there's one formula you need to memorize and implement if you want to be successful in relationships.

Romantics encourage the idea that when you find the right person, that person completes you and makes you whole. This philosophy might make you feel soft and warm inside, but it doesn't play out well in life. And it certainly isn't biblical.

If you had to put this philosophy into a mathematical formula, it would be $\frac{1}{2} + \frac{1}{2} = 1$. Sure, this works when learning simple fractions, but not when forming a healthy dating relationship! How effective is it to choose someone who meets your needs and wants when your needs and wants change on a daily basis? How smart is it to choose someone that matches who you are today when you will be a different you within three months?

Let's leave that formula in your textbooks and look to Biblical Math for a better option. According to Scripture, the winning equation for a God-honoring relationship is $1 + 1 = 1$.

> **1 WHOLE, HEALTHY PERSON + 1 WHOLE, HEALTHY PERSON = 1 WHOLE, HEALTHY RELATIONSHIP**

How can this be?! In the beginning, God had a big reveal party with creation. He rolled out breathtaking sunsets, majestic mountains, and crashing ocean waves. He went big and added giraffes, hippos, and sloths. But He waited until the very end to make His best creation – us.

Then God said, "Let us make man in our image, after our likeness. And let them have dominion over the fish of the sea and over the birds of the heavens and over the livestock and over all the earth and over every creeping thing that creeps on the earth." So God created man in His own image, in the image of God He created him; male and female He created them. (Genesis 1:26-27)

As humans, we were created in the image of the God of the Universe. Let that sink in for a minute. So many qualities that God carries in Himself were infused into us as we were created—compassion, creativity, intellect, reason, and the desire to be in relationships. If you need more proof of our individual wholeness, read Psalm 139:13-16. David writes to be sure we understand we are created with purpose and on purpose.

As an individual, if you are in Christ, you are whole and complete, lacking nothing. Right now. You don't need anything or any person to complete you. You are already complete. A romantic relationship is simply a bonus, an extra from God to add to your already fulfilled life.

If you want to be in a healthy relationship, your first step is to live in that wholeness. Work on being the best 1 you can be. Be confident in who God has made you to be. Celebrate your uniqueness. Be comfortable in your own skin. Like yourself.

You know plenty of your friends who have not attended to step one. Instead, they seek to find someone that makes them feel whole, complete, confident, and liked. You also know that it never ends well. Most young adults will need to spend a solid amount of time on step one, usually more than they want to.

The second step, which can seem as intense as step one, is to find someone who is doing the same kind of self-work. Another passionate follower of Jesus who sees himself or herself as whole and complete, lacking nothing.

When you add these two intentional 1s together, you will meet the goal of "1 whole, healthy relationship." A relationship with Jesus at the center (not based solely on physical attraction), bringing out the best in both, and honoring all involved. (And you don't even need a calculator!)

As you reflect on this new formula, take a moment to journal your thoughts on each of these three elements. What does it look like to have Jesus at the center, bring out the best in someone else, and honor everyone involved?

HOW FULL IS YOUR CEREAL BOWL?

Do you like it when your parent answers "Yes!" to your requests?

Can I go to the movies tonight? Yes! Can I have money from you to pay for the movie? Yes! Can we get a puppy? Yes! Can I take the car tonight? Yes! (*Disclaimer: This can only be a legit yes if you're a licensed driver; otherwise, there are some legal issues!) We don't know of any teenager who hasn't loved it when a parent says "Yes!" to a passionate plea! But we also know that teenagers don't think it happens often enough... What if it could happen more? What if you could actually influence how often your parents respond positively to your requests? Would you be willing to do what it takes on your end?

It's all about trust. If your parents trust you, they're more likely to give you a yes. If they trust that what you say is true...if they trust you'll be where you say you'll be...if they trust you'll do what you say you'll do (without them having to remind you five times!), they're more likely to give you a yes.

And despite popular belief, trust is not a right. It's a privilege. Trust is something that needs to be earned and kept. So, how are you doing at earning and keeping your parents' trust?

Earning trust can look like this:

The empty bowl represents the trust you have with your parents. The bowl filled with yummy, sugary cereal represents all the opportunities you have to earn the trust of your parents. With each trust opportunity you take, you add to the trust bowl.

Circle four actions you could take this week to earn the trust of your parents:

- **Getting yourself out of bed in the morning**

- **Walking the dog (AND picking up the poop!)**

- **Putting your dishes in the sink or washer**

- **Asking "How can I help?"**

- **Being kind to your siblings**

- **Answering their texts right away**

- **Saying thank you for rides, food, and a roof over your head**

- **Keeping your room clean (or cleaning it for the first time in your life)**

- **Agreeing to their screen time rules**

- **Owning a mistake and saying you're sorry**

Each time you choose to do one of these actions, you're adding to the trust bowl. Just for fun, make an arrow from the full bowl to the empty bowl and draw some cereal in that trust bowl. With every positive choice you make, you add to the trust bowl.

Here's the truth: Life with a full trust bowl is a good life! It always has been—check out this verse from the Old Testament:

Honor your father and mother, that your days may be long in the land that the Lord your God is giving you. (Exodus 20:12)

It's the first commandment in the Bible with a promise—there's got to be something to that! Why do you think God did it that way?

Here's the cool thing about committing to filling the trust bowl with your parents—it doesn't just benefit you. It honors your parents, pleases God, and makes life better for everyone.

ASK GOD WHAT IT WOULD LOOK LIKE FOR YOU TO HONOR YOUR FATHER OR MOTHER TODAY. It might start with asking for forgiveness from God and your parent for the times in the last few weeks you haven't been honoring. Then, be open to what God might show you and write it down here.

WHAT NEEDS TO STOP AND WHAT NEEDS TO START?

God gave humans five senses to interpret life. They're all great, but most people have their favorite. Rank your favorite senses from 1 to 5:

___ **SIGHT**

___ **HEARING**

___ **TASTE**

___ **SMELL**

___ **TOUCH**

Senses are intended to help us enjoy life as God intended. For fun, add your favorite "good" thing that helps you enjoy each sense. Under "smell," you could write "cookies in the oven" or "freshly mowed grass." Beneath "sight," you might write "Grand Canyon" or "sunset over the ocean."

Our senses absorb so much every day! Sometimes, what we take in is beyond our control, like when you walk into the ripe smells of a locker room during P.E. Still, we usually do have quite a bit of control over what we see, hear, taste, smell, and feel. Even if something is offensive, you can choose to remove yourself from it or focus your attention away from it.

What we allow our senses to experience matters to God.
- What you listen to matters to God.
- What you look at matters to God.
- What you speak about matters to God.
- What you choose to touch matters to God.
- What you take into your lungs matters to God.

It matters to Him because what you take in from the outside impacts you on the inside. You may not want to believe that, so think about the last time you swallowed some bad chicken, nasty taco meat, contaminated veggies, or a pepper that was hotter than you thought. You ate it (not understanding it was bad), and something happened inside your stomach (which made you clearly understand that it was "bad").

> "Dating growing up was always hard. I was in love with Jesus, no matter what. I remember talking to a boy about my boundaries, then feeling like he wanted nothing to do with me after that. Jesus reminded me that He had a man for me who would honor me and respect my boundaries."
> - Ella, 24

Now, consider how when you eat healthy food it strengthens you. Generally, our bodies respond differently to fresh fruit than processed carbs. What goes in either fuels us or fattens us.

Jesus talked about this value during His famous Sermon on the Mount:

***The eye is the lamp of the body. So, if your eye is healthy, your whole body will be full of light, but if your eye is bad, your whole body will be full of darkness. If then the light in you is darkness, how great is the darkness!* (Matthew 6:22-23)**

So, are your senses bad? Not at all! Your senses are great, God-given tools, but when you misuse them, you can slip into bad territory.

Tracking so far? We're about to level up this conversation.

When you're a tween or teen, your body, mind, and feelings are on overload, all while you're also being given more freedom about what you want to focus on. That kind of independence is exciting, so you might start making your own music playlists, choose apps for your phone, taste your way to a new favorite Boba Tea, set up a Netflix watchlist, throw on a new wardrobe, or buy a particular scent for your underarms (ew, but true). It can be incredibly fun to broaden what your senses take in.

The catch? How we explore our senses also affects others. Maybe you've seen teenage guys randomly dogpile on each other to get out some energy, or some teenage girls hog a camera to get the perfect picture. Again, this can be innocent fun...or really frustrating to others.

Take that same value further. What happens when a friend puts their dirty feet up on your bed? How do you handle someone in a dating relationship who wants to be hugged *all* the time? What do you do when someone you value wants to show you explicit photos or porn? Can you say for certain how you'd respond if a person you're really into wants to kiss you…and kiss you longer…and get you to lie down as they kiss you…and keep letting their senses have their way?

What needs to stop, and what needs to start? God wants to help you figure that out:

But I say, walk by the Spirit, and you will not gratify the desires of the flesh. For the desires of the flesh are against the Spirit, and the desires of the Spirit are against the flesh, for these are opposed to each other, to keep you from doing the things you want to do. (Galatians 5:16-17)

Living by the Spirit means you don't live by a moral code that you change based on the moment. Living by the Spirit means consistently operating out of your relationship with God inside of you. It might help if you ask Him some specific questions and consider His already-written answers:

"GOD, WHEN IS SOMETHING A GREEN LIGHT?" God created you to be a relational person, so it's absolutely fine to express interest in some one. We do this by noticing him or her, looking into that person's eyes, and having a conversation. We then build the relationship through time, talks, and texts. Maybe we enter into that fun phase where we affectionately slap a buddy on the back or give a friend a side hug.

Amos 3:3 says, *"Do two walk together, unless they have agreed to meet?"* If our goal is to love God and express His kindness to someone, we're likely in the green zone. When our touches become about us, the light may be changing.

"GOD, WHEN IS SOMETHING A YELLOW LIGHT?" When you see a yellow light in traffic, do you speed up or slow down? While some may hit the gas, the actual intent of a yellow light is to get you to slow down so you don't hit a red light. That may not be what you see or do, though.

The same is true spiritually – Ephesians 4:17-19 instructs you not to lose your sensitivity and floor it to "practice every kind of impurity." Likewise, Ephesians 5:3 adds, *"But sexual immorality and all impurity or covetousness must not even be named among you."* What might that be in a friendship when someone tries to get you to drift away from God? What happens when dating turns to touching, kissing, or using the word "love" to accelerate the relationship – should it, or should you slow down so you don't hit a red light?

"GOD, WHEN IS SOMETHING A RED LIGHT?" Marriage is incredible, and some things are only meant for it. If you're crossing lines sexually in any form of sex, it's an obvious red light. God's biggest teaching on this, though, isn't just "Don't have sex until you're married."

Hebrews 13:4 spells out a deeper value: **"Let marriage be held in honor among all, and let the marriage bed be undefiled, for God will judge the sexually immoral and adulterous."** The takeaway? Honor marriage…and even the marriage bed.

So, might that also include sleeping next to each other? If you do that, how are you watering down the joy of cuddling in bed for the first time with your future spouse? Also consider Proverbs 6:27, which says, **"Can a man carry fire next to his chest and his clothes not be burned?"** If you're trying to prove you can lay down next to someone you're attracted to without anything ever happening, you're ignoring this warning…and ignoring God's warning is an automatic red light.

Remember, the point of these questions isn't to grab the loudest morals in the room (even if that room is inside a church building). It's about being honest with God's desires for you, asking Him the questions, and studying what He's already said. When you do, you're bringing light into your body to fill you and reset your "sense" of things. Ask Him, even now, "How's my driving?" Write what you hear from the Lord as you ask Him this question.

HOW IS IT ABSOLUTELY OKAY NOT TO DATE?

Listen to this…don't just skip past this page. Are you ready?

Your singleness is so, so incredibly significant. It has off-the-charts value to you, to others, and to God. Whether you're single now or one day will be (we'll get to that in a moment), or you're completely into being friends with the opposite gender and aren't looking to date right now, know that it's absolutely fine for you to not be dating someone. You are remarkable, incredible, and exceptionally loved by God, and you have tremendous worth whether or not you have someone on your arm. Got it?

When you were little, you probably started rolling around in a crib one day. Eventually, you did more – likely crawling, standing up, and wobbling your way to your first steps. There was a first word you said, too. Hopefully, it was a good one, like "Dadda" or "Momma" (versus "Jabberwocky").

These types of things don't happen the exact same way as others your age. Maybe they were running while you were stumbling. Perhaps you started singing while they were mumbling. It could be that you or a friend had some hur-

"DATING AND MARRIAGE DON'T SOLVE THE QUESTION OF LONELINESS."

dles physically or developmentally. We all have our own path in life physically, and that uniqueness doesn't make you or them more or less significant, right? God wants you free from anxiety about someone else's path so you can fully step into your path.

But did you know that this is also true relationally? As you look at your peers today, it's tempting to compare how they're developing differently in friendships or dating. Maybe they're super social, and you aren't (or vice-versa). It could be they're incredibly at ease with others of the opposite gender, and you're still trying to say your first word to them (hint: don't make it "Jabberwocky.") We all have our own path in life relationally, and that uniqueness doesn't make you or them more or less significant, okay? God wants you free from anxiety about someone else's path so you can fully step into your path. Check out what the Apostle Paul was inspired by God to write down on this

"To the unmarried and the widows I say that it is good for them to remain single, as I am. But if they cannot exercise self-control, they should marry. For it is bet-ter to marry than to burn with passion...I want you to be free from anxieties. The unmarried man is anxious about the things of the Lord, how to please the Lord.

But the married man is anxious about worldly things, how to please his wife, and his interests are divided. And the unmarried or betrothed woman is anxious about the things of the Lord, how to be holy in body and spirit. But the married woman is anxious about worldly things, how to please her husband. I say this for your own benefit, not to lay any restraint upon you, but to promote good order and to secure your undivided devotion to the Lord." (1 Corinthians 7:8-9, 32-35)

Don't assume the main point here is that singleness is better than being married. There's actually a lot in that same chapter and other passages about how marriage is also a holy thing. Both singleness and marriage matter and connect to the path you're on with God. The purpose of your singleness, dating, friendships, and future marriage is all the same – honor God with every part of your life.

Isn't that the better takeaway? Just as a marriage reflects the love Jesus has for the Church, singleness reflects the love someone has for God. Don't assume someone is more spiritual based on their relationship status. Whichever path is or isn't yours right now or for the long haul is for you to be "free from anxieties" about.

It's just not that easy some days, though, is it? If you believe life is "second-rate" when you're single, you'll sink into a funk. Feeling lonely or not pursued can be a very real, heart-breaking challenge. As you see others in relationships or don't get vibes back from someone you're vibing on, you might wonder if you're invisible to them…to others…to God.

Maybe you've been told to "enjoy your single season" by others. Perhaps you've been told to pray and that you shouldn't feel lonely because "you have God." That can add a whole lot of guilt on top of how you're already feeling because you've never felt content not being in a relationship.

From the depths of our hearts, know that we can relate, and it's not just because we each had a season of singleness before dating the person we married but because we've learned a valuable lesson across singleness and dating/marriage. Dating and marriage don't solve the question of loneliness. The Apostle Paul also noted what God told him during a personal struggle, *"But He said to me, 'My grace is sufficient for you, for my power is made perfect in weakness.' Therefore I will boast all the more gladly of my weaknesses, so that the power of Christ may rest upon me." (2 Corinthians 12:9)*

What if you use whatever season you're in to let God make you whole? After all, even having someone in your life isn't permanent. One day, you or that person will likely be single again – if you're dating, things may not work out. If you do get married, one of you may pass away before the other. Singleness is a part of life. That's why God's ideal for any friendship or dating relationship is for two individually whole people to create something whole with Him together.

- **ASKING > ASSUMING:** If you assume God is overlooking you, don't bottle that up. Have the courage to ask Him if that's true and receive His answer. He's already written it down: Psalm 139:14, Psalm 147:3, Isaiah 41:10, Zephaniah 3:17, 1 John 3:1, and 1 John 4:9-10.

- **BECOMING > BLAMING:** Is there something "off" about who you are? Absolutely. That's true of everyone. Don't miss this – no one is smooth all the time (even those who can pull off saying "Jabberwocky"). Instead of blaming life when you're feeling awkward, find your God-given "thing" that nurtures life and confidence. You might, in this season, discover that you're a writer, kid's ministry volunteer, cook, musician, runner, missionary, or the best local pickleball player. Do those things with God, telling Him what you enjoy about it and thanking Him for letting you find it.

- **CONTENTMENT > COMPANIONSHIP:** What would you want your life to be like if you never dated or got married? That could be a hard question, but let yourself go there. If you knew this was your path, what would you do to thrive and not just survive? As you take the time to consider this, know that you're onto something huge – that God wants you to have a fulfilling relationship with Him and yourself without having to involve another person. If you do end up in a dating relationship, you're that much more solid going into it... and if you don't date, you're that much more solid without needing to date. Dream up what this could look like!

- **DOING > DREADING:** Alright, it's time to step into this. If you sense a calling to singleness for a season or the long haul, then "BOOM! DO IT!" and don't wait for a lightning bolt in the sky as a sign. If you hope to use this time of being single to be ready for a relationship in the future, then "BOOM! DO IT!" Ditch the bad habits and start some amazing habits. Bust out a journal and use it to express gratitude to God for who He is and what's happening in your life.

Remember, God doesn't promise dating or marriage to everyone, so don't idolize it. Likewise, being single doesn't magically

As I wrestled with how to approach marriage and dating when I was younger, I recognized the Lord was calling me to remain single for the sake of His ministry and I've followed that calling since. This singleness has been a gift in a lot of ways - I have more availability to say yes to things, can make spontaneous decisions, and don't have to worry about trying to impress anyone. On the flip side, I have to be more intentional in investing in friendships to ensure I have someone to talk to and in monitoring my behavior. Even so, singleness has been a tremendous gift, and I am thankful I have remained faithful to the Lord's calling.
- Daniel, 20

complete you, so don't idolize it either. You're developing differently than others, and God wants you free from anxiety about someone else's path so you can fully step into your path *"For He satisfies the longing soul, and the hungry soul He fills with good things."* **(Psalm 107:9)**

How will you choose to step into all of this?

HOW DO YOU RECOVER?
MISTAKES 1.0

Are you 16 yet?

Most teenagers can't wait until they get their driver's license when they turn 16. When you have your license, you have more freedom, responsibility, and another place to crank your music without your mom telling you to turn it down. The written driver's test can be a challenge, and the behind-the-wheel test will prove to be one of the most stressful experiences of your life. But it's totally worth it!

One aspect of driving that instructors don't spend a lot of time on is the speed bump. Sure, there are other important elements like seat belts, highway driving, and being a defensive driver, but speed bumps should be bumped up on the list! Think about it, if you don't handle a speed bump well, you can get stuck in the school parking lot or ruin the underside of your Toyota Corolla.

The same is true for mistakes we make in life. Like speed bumps, mistakes are an inevitable reality. The question isn't whether or not you'll find them; the question is how will you handle them.

Just for fun, describe the first mistake you remember making in life that got you in trouble (think punching your sister from your car seat, stealing candy from the store, or swearing at your mom).

As a teenager, you may find yourself making more mistakes than you did in past years. Don't worry about it – it's all part of the growing-up process. However, learning how to move through those mistakes is vital.

Think of it like a speed bump. The primary purpose of a speed bump is to slow you down. Many people don't get that—they don't slow down at all, which bottoms out their car, or they come to a complete stop, which makes clearing the speed bump difficult. The best way to handle a speed bump is to slow down, move carefully through it, and accelerate up to a normal speed on the other side.

So, you cheat on a math test and get caught. Your teacher is disappointed. Your parents are confused and angry. You feel like you let everyone down. Even in that hard moment, you have a choice. You can choose to fly by the issue so it'll be over, you can have your life come to a screeching halt, or you can choose to move through the consequences and accelerate on a path of better choices.

The Bible has a lot to say about how we should handle our mistakes and failures. In fact, we are promised this: "If we confess our sins, He is faithful and just to forgive us our sins and to cleanse us from all unrighteousness." (1 John 1:9)

God's promise is true, and we can count on it!

Why should we stay stuck in guilt over our mistakes when God is willing to wipe them clean? He does allow us to experience the consequences of our mistakes in hopes that we won't make those same mistakes again, but His forgiveness is what allows us to move through that speed bump in life and onto a better road ahead.

You might be thinking, "What does it look like to move through the speed bump/consequences?" Great question! Just follow these "simple" steps:

1. Admit what you did and that it was wrong.
2. Be willing to accept whatever consequences are given.
3. Don't complain about the consequences or blame anyone else for your mistake.
4. Commit to yourself that you will learn from your mistake and not do it again.
5. Leave it behind and move forward with confidence and humility.

Take a moment and look at those steps again. Knowing yourself, circle the step that would be the hardest for you to take. Below, write two reasons why that step would be hard for you:

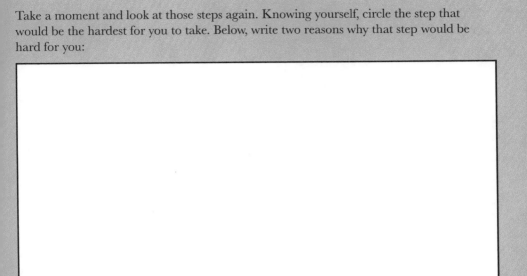

HERE'S THE TRUTH: You will be driving over speed bumps for the rest of your life. You will also make mistakes for the rest of your life. Are you willing, with both, to slow down, keep moving and accelerate into a better road ahead?

EXPERIENCE: MISTAKES 2.0

Did you know it can take five minutes to gain a reputation and five years to lose it? In our world, that's just kind of how it is.

In a weak moment, you take a drink at a party, and now everyone thinks you're a "drinker." You send a photo you didn't want to send or let your guard down in a back bedroom with someone, and now you're "easy" or a "player." You struggle to learn and need help in a class everyone else aced, and now you're "stupid." You were abused by your older cousin, and now you're an "abused" child.

In our world, what you do allegedly makes you who you are.

ALLEGEDLY.

Have you ever heard that when Jesus came, He turned our world upside down? That His Kingdom is an "upside-down" Kingdom? Think about it. Jesus said things like, "The last shall be first, the first shall be last"…"love your enemies."…"forgive those who persecute you"…"have faith like a child." What?!

In Jesus' Kingdom, you are not defined by what you do. You are defined by Who loves you and what He did for you.

Because of this, God will take anything that you have done or that has been done to you, and He will make good out of it. The Apostle Paul reminds us of this in Romans 8:28, *"And we know that for those who love God all things work together for good, for those who are called according to His purpose."*

It's true that your past will affect you. Just like we talked about in the last devotional, there is an extent to which you'll need to own your mistakes. God allows consequences for our sins in hopes that we will be motivated to avoid those choices in the future. If we allow Him to make good out of our not-so-good decisions, though, He will!

But what about the choices that are made against us? We live in a sinful and broken world, and bad choices don't only affect the person making them. Unfortunately, some

> **IN JESUS' KINGDOM, YOU ARE NOT DEFINED BY WHAT YOU DO. YOU ARE DEFINED BY WHO LOVES YOU AND WHAT HE DID FOR YOU.**

choose poorly, and others are hurt in the process. People choose to act violently, abuse, take revenge, and steal. Those choices hurt others. Those choices affect others. But the poor choices people have made that have hurt you don't have to define you!

Have you ever heard about the life of Joseph in the book of Genesis? You can read the whole saga in Genesis 37-50, but here's the recap—Joseph grew up as the second youngest of a lot of brothers and had quite a bit of confidence. His brothers got tired of him being their dad's favorite, and they didn't want to hear any more of his dreams where everyone bowed down to him. So, they threw him into a pit and sold him to slavers, who took him to Egypt. (And you thought YOU had issues with your brothers and sisters?!) Even though Joseph's brothers chose poorly, God made good out of those choices. He gave Joseph favor in the eyes of people in high positions, and Joseph ended up, years later, as the second in command over all of Egypt. A famine in the land brought everyone to Egypt to get food. When Joseph's brothers realized who the man in charge was, they were certain he would kill them for what they had done to him years before. Check out how Joseph responds:

"But Joseph said to them, 'Do not fear, for am I in the place of God? As for you, you meant evil against me, but God meant it for good, to bring it about that many people should be kept alive, as they are today.'" (Genesis 50:19-20)

Aren't you glad you can live in Jesus' upside-down Kingdom? A world where good can come out of bad? A world where my past affects me, but it doesn't define me?

Take a few minutes to thank God for how He makes things good for those who love Him. Fill this entire space up, talking directly to God and being open to hearing His voice as you do.

Finally, share what you experienced in taking the time to do this.

EVER NOTICE HOW MANY "HOT PEOPLE" NEED JESUS?

Sure, you do. Other people do, too. That's why "missionary dating" exists. It's when a solid Christian guy or girl says, "I feel the Lord calling me to make sure a certain gloriously good-looking person I know gets saved, and the only way that can happen is if we date and I dare them to come to church or else it's totally over, but not really, because they're so gorgeous that I'm sure Jesus doesn't want me to give up on them."

Hey, if you haven't seen this yet, you probably will. Hopefully, you won't fall for it.

Attraction can't be the basis of a relationship. At best, it can maybe give you a reason to get to know who someone really is…but just know that because you're attracted to him or her, you're going to filter everything they say and do as if it's all good. In a way, you'll have blinders on when it comes to other things they say and do because they're so attractive.

This temptation isn't anything new, and many ancient cultures have tried to remedy this through "arranged marriages." This is where a mom, dad, extended family, or local matchmaker (usually seen in movies as an old lady with a thick accent who wears long scarves and drinks tea) would try to make sure that whomever you married was a "good match." In this way, the people who loved you and knew you best would use their experience and wisdom to help you find someone who would be amazing for you in a marriage that could last and thrive in the years to come.

ATTRACTION CAN'T BE THE BASIS OF A RELATIONSHIP.

Sure, some families didn't matchmake or arrange marriages for reasons that honored God. When they did, though, the couple who was brought together wasn't just basing their future marriage on feelings inside their body or external appearances but on deeper values that really matter.

What's one thing you wouldn't like about this?

_____

What's one thing you would really appreciate about this?

_____

If your parents were to choose someone for you now, who do you think they would choose?

One good example of this in the Bible is when an old dad named Abraham wanted his twenty-something-year-old son Isaac to have a great wife. Abraham put his servant on the job and told him:

"That I may make you swear by the Lord, the God of heaven and God of earth, that you will not take a wife for my son from the daughters of the Canaanites, among whom I dwell…The Lord, the God of heaven, who took me from my father's house and from the land of my kindred, and who spoke to me and swore to me, 'To your offspring I will give this land,' He will send His angel before you, and you shall take a wife for my son from there. But if the woman is not willing to follow you, then you will be free from this oath of mine; only you must not take my son back there." (Genesis 24:3, 7-8)

That seems like quite a journey! Why not have Isaac just marry some attractive local woman who had different beliefs about God and life? And for that matter, why not just send Isaac to the Promised Land to find the first woman he's attracted to?
What do you think? Why does any of this matter?

Notice that if the woman didn't want to come back, she didn't have to. Even in match-making, God is a fan of choice and free will. Why might this matter, too?

Now, try to personalize this. Even if you're more into the idea of modern dating, what might God want you to pay attention to here? Like, are you someone who wants to be in absolute control of your dating life or base it on attraction at the expense of something greater? Or, are you open to deeper values and wisdom on what makes a relationship work? Who in your life would you let speak into you about anyone you'd be friends with or date? How much healthier could those areas of your life be if you sought out people who followed God, who helped you seek out other people?

When God is in the equation, you don't have to live in desperation.

WRITE A PRAYER OUT TO GOD HERE:

Even if you'd never want your family to arrange a marriage for you, what would it mean for you to open up to God as Someone who knows better than you do and is looking out for your best?

IS IT A FLAW OR A FLAG?

Are you a fan of thrifting? How do you feel about purchasing items with a bit of wear and tear that were previously owned by someone else but are still in decent condition? You could snag a great deal on a dream vehicle or stylish clothes with minor imperfections you can live with.

These are called flaws.

Now imagine that item falls apart after a week! You could try a hack to fix it, but what if it keeps collapsing? Do you keep pouring time and money into it? When do you ask, "Is this even good?"

These are called flags.

Everyone has flaws, including you. Sometimes, they're publicly obvious – like a small scar where a cat scratched you or if your nose tilts a little more one way than another. Other flaws are assumed, like if you discover someone is into country music (YIKES!) and you're not. These differences in looks and tastes are just that – differences…nothing more. Any value about them comes from our personal preferences, like if we say, "I don't mind his Northern accent, except when he calls a 'bag' a 'beeeeg,'" or "Why doesn't she wave at me when she's running track and handing off her baton?"

A flaw is a difference or preference in the person or relationship, but not harmful. It's just chemistry, and it can be talked through.

A flag, on the other hand, is something someone does that depletes you and gives you a reason to question the whole relationship. It's about compatibility, and it needs more than talk – it requires change.

Some flags are easily noticeable. For example, does that person yell, dishonor boundaries, badmouth others, criticize your parents, ignore you, skip out on plans, or give gifts so you overlook bad behavior? These are flags, for sure.

It's just that other, not-so-noticeable flags also exist, like generally being on edge in the relationship. We may say, "She isn't trying to hurt me," or, "He said he's working on this," but just because a person isn't actively harmful doesn't necessarily mean the relationship is helpful.

Jesus warned us to not be influenced by others without first examining their character. In this passage, He's referring to leaders or prophets, but it also can apply to anyone in our lives.

"Beware of false prophets, who come to you in sheep's clothing but inwardly are ravenous wolves. You will recognize them by their fruits. Are grapes gathered from thornbushes, or figs from thistles? So, every healthy tree bears good fruit, but the diseased tree bears bad fruit. A healthy tree cannot bear bad fruit, nor can a diseased tree bear good fruit. Every tree that does not bear good fruit is cut down and thrown into the fire. Thus you will recognize them by their fruits." (Matthew 7:15-20)

What could you notice here? Write a few observations that could help you in your relationships.

Sometimes we develop "tunnel vision" where we focus so much on the person we're dating that we ignore the perspective around us. I love the imagery from Ecclesiastes 4:12 of how a "threefold cord is not easily broken." If you and the person you're dating are two of these cords, who is your third? Who will support and challenge you as you grow? Asking this will help you honestly look inward, direct it upwards to God, as you move forward.
-Joshua, 23

Every relationship in your life will have flaws. Most will also occasionally have a quick appearance of a flag when someone hurts the other person on accident or out of a bad mood. Other relationships, though, are always flying a flag. Ask good questions to discover your situation:

- **WHAT IS MY COMMITMENT TO THIS PERSON?** Consider how a married couple made a covenant with God to work things out "for better or for worse." New friends or a new couple, though, aren't under the same commitment and can absolutely end something full of hurtful flags or incompatible flaws. Long-term connections may feel trickier with all your history, but don't let a few years of being with this person obligate you to decades more of the same.

- **ARE THINGS PRIMARILY HEALTHY WITH THE OCCASIONAL AWKWARD MOMENT?** Or is it primarily awkward with the occasional healthy moment? Be honest. Ask others around you, and don't debate what they share. You may not want them to be right, but ignoring your trend is wrong.

- **DOES THE OTHER PERSON QUOTE JESUS OR OVERFLOW WITH JESUS?** When we're interested in someone, we tend to look for any hint that they're on board with our deepest values. They can pick up on this and say what we're hoping to hear so we don't push them away as a friend or date. What if you genuinely evaluated what's coming out of their lives? What kind of relationship is he or she actually capable of with you if you really are putting God first in every area of your life?

- **WHAT IS THIS PERSON DOING TODAY WITH THE PAST?** What happened to a person in the past can affect what's happening in a person right now. For example, someone could come from a family where everyone yells at each other. That's just a flaw if this person has noticed it and chosen to instead be kind. If that person recklessly yells, though, and says, "That's just how I was raised," then that's a flag.

- **HAVE I DRAWN LINES, AND WILL I HONOR THEM?** As best as you can, know what a flag is before you get into a relationship so you don't react based on feelings or attachment. Decide how you'll handle a friend who always begs for money, refuses to pay for things, smokes, swears, watches questionable movies, shouts, threatens, has poor hygiene, gossips, never says "thank you," or makes a mess of your things. What if someone you date flirts or cheats with others, tries to get you to lower your physical standards, threatens self-harm if you break up, never helps you with things, or criticizes the type of family you want someday?

- **WHO IS THE SAVIOR IN THIS RELATIONSHIP?** When there's trouble, do you first turn to Jesus or to each other? Sure, the right answer is "Jesus." Is that the actual answer, though?

Bottom line? Don't settle for bad friends or sad dates out of insecurity. Consider the thrift store metaphor – we've all "belonged" to others and might show signs of wear, yet still be in decent shape.

Take a moment and ask God to speak to you about what's important in someone you'd be a friend to or date. Write it down here. Then, look at your list and circle anything you'll agree with Him on and live out, including not settling for flags He doesn't want you to settle on. What does He have for you?

WHAT ARE YOU UNAWARE OF?

Years ago, a popular theme park advertised a special effects show to teach how things happen behind the scenes in movies. The attraction didn't post a warning about content, so adults and kids alike poured in to see demonstrations of different make-up and movie effects that didn't necessarily filter the presentation for younger audiences. Every show allowed kids to see multiple graphic horror movie scenes and watch an audience member be "cut" by a knife (not knowing the prop and blood were fake). At a certain point in the show, kids were asked if the host should shoot a monster with his gun, and if they thought so, they should chant together, "Shoot it! Shoot it! Shoot it!"

What would you do if you were in the middle of that show and saw this taking place? Would you think, "Well, that's just the world we're in," or wonder, "Should we be doing this? What if I spoke up?" Perhaps another question might be, "Should I even be in here? What am I affirming?" Consider what Paul has to say here from Romans:

"Do not be conformed to this world, but be transformed by the renewal of your mind, that by testing you may discern what is the will of God, what is good and acceptable and perfect...I want you to be wise as to what is good and innocent as to what is evil." (Romans 12:2, 16:19b)

A big value God is trying to tell us through these verses is that we need to notice the pattern of the world so we don't just fold into it. Instead, we get to live differently by letting God change the way we think, so instead of tolerating evil, we choose to step away from it in all its forms. This does include checking ourselves and what we participate in. Take stock of how you may have inherited some of this:

- The time you get off from school during the Christmas season used to generally be known as Christmas Break. Over the years, it's become more known as Winter Break to not offend others. Is that okay? Or should we as Christians reclaim that it's Christmas Break?

- It used to be that when a guy dated a girl, she was the "girlfriend," and he was the "boyfriend." A married man was a husband, and a married woman was a wife. Now that the world is very opinionated and divided about gender, the word "partner" is being used. Is that okay? Or should we, as Christians, not use the word "partner" but instead recognize God's design for relationships by using gender-specific words?

- The language of "same-sex" and "marriage" has been put together as a legal relationship option in our world. Meanwhile, that isn't what God describes marriage to be (see Matthew 19, Ephesians 5, Hebrews 13). If we use that phrase out loud, are we affirming something that doesn't exist in His Kingdom? Is that okay? Or should we, as Christians, not put words in front of "marriage" that confuse what "marriage" actually, biblically, and foundationally is?

- Kids' movies used to be pretty clean options for families to watch, but now, instead of them simply being entertainment, many movies try to make a stand for something through language and content that pushes certain ideas. Is that okay? Or are kids being groomed into content and ideologies that take them away from fully trusting in God and His plans?

How does your language reflect cultural values over biblical ones? How might you accidentally be endorsing something God wants you to walk away from? Which influencers are influencing you, and now that you think about it (and pray about it), should they be? What do you not know you're being made aware of?

This is an incredibly hard time to grow up. All of this is so subtle as if everyone in the world is saying, "It doesn't matter if you should know this or if you're meant to process this. We're going to give it to you right now to get you thinking about it, saying it, and promoting it."

So, how does that impact your ideas on singleness, dating, friendship, and romance? Before you answer that, know this: God sees you. God knows you. God calls you great things. He persists in what is good, and wants your persistence in what is good. He'll help you learn, grow, and change from the inside out.

But you have to decide if you'll agree with Him above all else or try to be a good citizen above all else. You have to choose to want different things than what this world says matters most. It's your choice to either fight the good fight and train for it or to coast on a salvation decision you made for Jesus, assuming it's all smooth sailing after that.

God has given you His words, so you don't have to guess about any of this. No one likes to be pruned, but everyone wants a fruitful life (which requires letting God hack off things that are stealing life from you). Perhaps that's the real issue here – we hate the blade, but we love the harvest.

> The world tells us to rush into dating. I think it's better to know the person for a while, like being friends in a group or colleagues at work. You shouldn't rush into a relationship but get to know the person for who they are and if they truly put God first in their life!
> - Noah, 18

You'll notice that on some of those cultural bullet points earlier, we didn't tell you, "Here's what you should do or say." Instead, we exposed a choice you have to make so you'd wrestle with God on it. He's the one who wants you to **"pray without ceasing...test everything; hold fast what is good. Abstain from every form of evil."** **(1 Thessalonians 5:17, 21-22)**

Will you choose to be in alignment with God...on everything?

Will you let Him change your thoughts so your words and actions match His, even if it means not using the same thinking and language as the world?

What has the world told you about dating and romance that you've bought into? How do you think it's "supposed to look" based on what you've been handed by people, books, and movies?

What do you expect friendship to be like in real life based on how fictional, well-scripted TV shows have portrayed it?

How do you think of singleness – have you been made to believe that you're supposed to go to the gym all the time or get a new wardrobe to become "hot" so you can "finally" get out of this season?

Write it down...What do you not know you're being made aware of?

WHAT ARE 5 QUALITIES CHRISTIAN GUYS ARE INTO?

Ladies, are you ready to spy on the brain of a Christian guy?

We can't put you on the Magic School Bus and shrink down for a school field trip inside his head. First of all, that's creepy…why would a teacher take students into weird places that a bus clearly isn't equipped to go?

Secondly, are you sure you'd want to get inside the brain of a Christian guy? What if it's everything awful you fear it actually is in there? Even scarier, what if the thoughts of that Christian guy are so incredible that it makes you feel you can't, as a female, live up to what he's thinking?

Well, we have good news for you – Christian guys are just as human as you. They've stepped into the grace of God, asked for His forgiveness, and are on a trajectory of growth to become more like Jesus. They've taken some steps, and they have many more steps to take.

This means they know how to extend grace to you while encouraging you to become all that God made you to be. If you're a Christian and are going to be in a relationship with a guy, God wants it to be with a Christian guy like this. Don't settle for less.

Wait…isn't this chapter supposed to be about the qualities Christian guys are into when it comes to girls? Absolutely. We just needed to establish what the question is actually asking. We're wondering what Christian guys are into…not what non-believing guys are into. If you're interested in that second question, well…let's take a crack at it. Despite the stereotypes, guys are more than their sex drive. Many of them set goals that they pursue in order to carve out whatever they sense manhood is. This could mean trying to dominate a sport, save up for a vehicle, get into a certain school, or do something meaningful…whatever that is.

That said, guys do biologically deal with a 24-hour cycle of testosterone that peaks and lowers throughout the day, making their sex drive naturally bounce all over the place. If a guy isn't genuinely being led by God and instead caving into cultural values, he'll likely be looking for a girl to find physical pleasure with. Without the Lord leading him, he may also play games to sort through the ladies he encounters so he can figure out which ones will satisfy him.

How do you feel about that? What if he's really, really attractive…but isn't following Christ?

Back to the original question – a healthy Christian guy isn't the last guy we described, nor is he merely a church attender. Lots of guys who are regularly at youth groups and week-end services may have a great habit of being there, but that doesn't mean they're all-in on Jesus.

How could you potentially tell the difference?

So now we're even clearer on how the question is about what a Christian guy is. Maybe now we can more accurately answer what is attractive to him. What would be so outstanding to a real man of God who could bless your life in ways you may actually hope for deep down?

The answer is obvious, isn't it?

Quality #1: You're a genuine Jesus-follower who's led by the Holy Spirit.

Christian guys are looking for you to be on the same spiritual journey they're on…as

they follow Jesus, they want to bump into you already following Him, too. That means they'll be watching to observe if you're the real deal – do you just talk the talk, or do you also walk the walk? *"But I say, walk by the Spirit, and you will not gratify the desires of the flesh." (Galatians 5:16)*

Quality #2: You're beautiful on the inside and outside.

This one may come with some baggage – yes, even Christian guys do see and consider your outside appearance. Thankfully, they're not focused on it in the same way guys who just follow their hormones are. They will simply feel or not feel chemistry with how you present yourself, and you don't need to worry about this. Rather, just invest in your body physically and develop your own epic style that lets you express on the outside who you are on the inside. Don't obsess over being "pretty" or "perfect," because a Christian guy knows there's more to be looking for. *"For while bodily training is of some value, godliness is of value in every way, as it holds promise for the present life and also for the life to come." (1 Timothy 4:8)*

Quality #3: You're living a life of purpose.

It's no secret that this world has lost people in it. Imagine a Christian guy's jaw dropping as he sees you doing something about it as God has created you to. Whether you boldly evangelize, serve kids, sing songs, dig dirt on mission trips, lead a Bible study, run tech, play an instrument, write inspiring things, or in your everyday life simply and regularly push back on the way things are, it's strikingly attractive to Jesus-following men! They adore watching you do the work of God! *"Charm is deceitful, and beauty is vain, but a woman who fears the Lord is to be praised." (Proverbs 31:30)*

Quality #4: You're willing to prune relationships.

Do you have friends who try to get you to settle for a less intense version of following Jesus? Might there be others in your life who try to get you to see yourself as less than how God does? A Christian guy is inspired when he sees you sort it out and not be influenced by the bad vibes, even if it means ending or changing those relationships. *"Do not be deceived: 'Bad company ruins good morals.'" (1 Corinthians 15:33)*

Quality #5: You're goofy and accessible.

It's refreshing for a Christian guy to see in the midst of all your godly stuff that you kind of nerd out about stuff. As long as he's not required to like all the things you like at the level you like it, this can be a really cute part of your relationship. So don't hide your goofiness, but let it be a bridge for him to know who you are. *"A joyful heart is good medicine, but a crushed spirit dries up the bones." (Proverbs 17:22)*

Hmm…maybe that last one means that Magic School Bus lady is onto something.

What is one of your favorite things about you? What might be one of God's favorite things?

WHAT ARE 5 QUALITIES CHRISTIAN GIRLS ARE INTO?

Girls are into a lot. Talking. Fashion. Romance. Smelling good. Make-up. Sports. Hair. Puppies. Leggings. Filters. And most of them are into guys long before guys are into them.

Once the guys catch up, what can they do to be the kind of guy a girl is into? What you see and hear in commercials, social media, movies, and shows can confuse you. It's about time you understand what a godly girl really wants.

You might want to have a dictionary next to you for this. Not because you don't have it in you but because these qualities aren't being defined or modeled well for young men in our culture.

God's desire and best for you starts with you being a passionate follower of Jesus. All the qualities young women of God want will be built on that foundational quality. It's a must. It's the base. A girl who is in love with Jesus won't take a second look at you unless you're also running toward Jesus with conviction. If you aren't sure how you land with this quality, take time to find a man of faith in your world—a youth leader, grandpa, neighbor, or cousin. It's a big deal.

If you can claim Jesus as your Lord and Savior, then it's time to start strengthening the qualities Christian girls are into. A few disclaimers: This list is not a complete list. More qualities could be added, but these make a great launching pad. If these aren't your best qualities right now, don't be discouraged. You will spend a good amount of your life working on these qualities, and that's okay, expected, and healthy. (In other words, many men in your life are still trying to secure these qualities at 50 years old!)

> "IF THESE AREN'T YOUR BEST QUALITIES RIGHT NOW, DON'T BE DISCOURAGED. YOU WILL SPEND A GOOD AMOUNT OF YOUR LIFE WORKING ON THESE QUALITIES, AND THAT'S OKAY, EXPECTED, AND HEALTHY."

Quality #1: Attentive

Being attentive means paying close attention to something or someone. This is a challenge for a young man because the options of what and who to pay attention to at any given moment of your day seem endless! When you are willing to block out all other options, you show the girls in your life that they matter to you.

Attentive guys don't just see girls; they notice a new haircut, a change in attitude, braces on/off, and who their best friends are. In a world where many of us don't feel seen or known, being attentive will set you apart!

Quality #2: Communicative

When you are communicative, you are ready to talk and ready to listen. You've probably noticed girls relate through talking. It makes sense, then, that they would want to relate to you by hearing you talk and having you listen to them.

You can strengthen your communication skills by making good eye contact, listening and not just hearing, and asking good questions. As you listen, you'll pick up on topics girls like to talk about. As you talk, they'll get to know what you're interested in. It's a great cycle to get into!

Quality #3: Expressive

Being expressive isn't just for the kids in theater and pageant queens; it's for smart guys. Showing emotion isn't weak, and it doesn't make you less than anyone else! An expressive person effectively conveys thoughts and feelings. It takes some work, but the results are worth it! When you thoughtfully consider what's in your head and heart and express them with words and facial expressions, you are giving a young woman insight into parts of you that seem hidden.

The first step to being expressive is to slow down enough to actually think about what you're thinking and feel what you're feeling. Most guys your age don't even consider slowing down, let alone work through thoughts and feelings. You will be exceptional!

Quality #4: Intentional

If you are an intentional person, you act with purpose. You are deliberate in your word choice, self-control, and actions. You are direct in your communication and advocate for what you need and the good of others. Girls love and appreciate guys who are intentional!

Quality #5: Self-aware

As you move through your teen years, you are starting to understand more about who you are and how you tick. Being self-aware means you also understand how others are impacted by you, plus you care about how you impact others, which means you're willing and open to change.

Girls appreciate a guy who understands his need for alone time—his tendency to be a know-it-all—his competitiveness—his anxiety—his love languages—and his solid work ethic. Take a personality inventory. Ask your parents what strengths you have. Watch for patterns in your behaviors. Get to know yourself so you can impact girls for good!

You might be thinking, where do I start?

1. Identify a trusted adult and ask for an evaluation of these five qualities in your life.
2. Pray through the results of the evaluation.
3. Find individuals with these qualities to stalk and copy their ways.
4. Practice. Practice. Practice.

Yes, it's overwhelming. Yes, it takes work. But yes, you're capable of pursuing all these qualities!

Which one of these qualities do you think you need the most growth in? How can you start bettering yourself today?

HOW DO YOU BECOME "ATTRACTIVE?"

What if we told you this chapter isn't going to be what you expect?

So let's get what you do expect out of the way.

Yes, the secret to becoming attractive absolutely involves you spending transformational time with Jesus. The person others are looking for as a friend, boyfriend, girlfriend, husband, wife…it's that individual who has authentically rooted himself or herself in the Lord. Just like a tree that's planted in good soil, sits in great proximity to the sun, and is watered well, you bear fruit when you're rooted in Christ.

"But the fruit of the Spirit is love, joy, peace, patience, kindness, goodness, faithfulness, gentleness, self-control; against such things there is no law." (Galatians 5:22-23)

"YOU'RE ALREADY LOVED BY GOD, AND HIS LOVE WILL TRANSFORM YOU INTO THE KIND OF PERSON WHO DOES THE RIGHT THINGS."

While this is a foundational first step, let's take a look at some practical advice. That's what you probably want anyway. So, based on a leading expert on how to become attractive, along with our own personal observations over the years on how certain people stand out, we'll give you the lowdown.

First, though, let's define "attraction" – this means there is something about you that draws others to you. We'll stay in the dating lane on this one, so what follows is primarily wisdom for that question. If you're feeling called to singleness, then you can read this for some wisdom to dish out. Then again, feel free to apply it as a friend and be that much more compelling socially.

TO BECOME A MORE ATTRACTIVE PERSON...

Radiate Worth

One thing we mistakenly believe about being attractive is that it requires Hollywood-level looks or fitness model muscles. That's a visual attraction bias that assumes if you notice such physical traits in others, it's what they're ultimately requiring of you. What's more accurate is that people are more deeply attracted to the charisma and worth they have concluded about themselves, and that swagger is way more interesting than insecurity. Want to develop this? Grow in your assurance that you have worth and radiate that worth.

Be Great Without A Relationship

Wanting to date is quite different than being deflated if you aren't dating. Living in such disappointment puts every potential person of the opposite gender on a pedestal that raises higher and higher the longer you aren't dating, making everyone you're interested in seem that much more out of reach. This pessimism is another filter that shrinks your perception of feeling attractive, and that leaks out of you. If you're instead smiling out of something incredible inside of you, no matter what, that's attractive.

Overcome Conflict

Life is full of drama, and people rarely step into it because of a fear that much more drama will happen. Rather than reconcile with people we struggle with, we ghost them out of cowardice. So imagine how impressive it is to be the kind of person who cuts through that and says, "No, we're going to work on this. I'm committed to doing my part, and I'm asking you to do your part."

Value Time

On one hand, don't be in a rush. Impatience implies insecurity, neediness, and unattractive desperation. On the other hand, be timely in how you reply to texts and conversations so you don't leave someone hanging. Not stressing when things aren't happening and honoring the time of others both demonstrate maturity. This is especially felt when you're connecting with others and are fully present with healthy eye contact, not giving them the feeling that you're in a rush to be somewhere else. Even if you only have five minutes to give, give them the best five minutes you can until you move on to other things.

Be Thoughtful

When someone feels noticed and remembered, it's one of the best kinds of flirting. This also has to be genuine, not selling yourself out of desperation. Instead, giving a special gift or serving them in a way that communicates understanding stands out. For example, "I remember you saying you had a long day ahead of you, so I brought you this smoothie," says, "What matters to you matters to me." Wow! That can be truly attractive.

Inspire Others

An old saying suggests that if you aren't standing for something, you'll fall for everything. Pick a good fight, and fight that good fight whether or not anyone joins in. In ancient times, men did this by being hunters who went out and fought for food for the family while women built a home for them to come back to. That's obviously dated, and we're not suggesting you should go fetch a quail for her or buy toilet paper for him. Rather, it's easy today to slip into gaming and scrolling. Having ambition shows that you actually care about something in a world where no one knows where to start, so try to figure out what that is for you. Value something and work hard at it. You'll stand out for good.

Show Up

Are you the type of person who shows up and cheers for things that are important to others? What about being a listening ear when someone is having a hard time? Don't cheat others out of your presence. Be there when it counts and even when it doesn't. Like a bank, lots of small, appropriate "investments" can create huge "interest."

Control Your Strength

Imagine one of those huge machines that junkyards use to crush cars, but instead of using its jaws to flatten metal, it's holding one single egg in its grip. Now, picture living this way – you have the personality and power to make things happen, but you're intentional about it. There can be a time for all your strength to be used, like when something bad is happening and needs to stop, especially if someone is being hurt or degraded. But even then, choose how you use your strength so that people appreciate your passion instead of fearing your wrath.

Choose the Greater "YES"

There are so many things that no one would fault you for doing or agreeing to, like saying yes when someone offers you a late-night sundae. If you were an Olympic athlete in training, though, you'd likely pass on it because you'd be saying a greater "YES" to something that mattered more. The real key is not merely knowing what's better but actually living this out sacrificially. Restraint isn't about saying no to everything but yes to greater things. In a dating relationship, it can keep you from throwing yourself at someone and instead valuing the right place and space for physical affection later on in God's greater context.

By this point, you might be thinking, "Okay, this is good advice, but where does God come in? Why'd we read that verse earlier if we're not gonna talk about it?" And that's where you're mistaken! That entire list is rooted in what we read earlier. We've been talking about it this whole time! The love of God is what gives you worth to radiate; the joy of God helps you be great without a relationship; the peace of God is what overcomes conflict; the patience of God guides you to value time; the kindness of God drives you to be thoughtful; the goodness of God picks the right fight that inspires others; the faithfulness of God prompts you to show up; the gentleness of God coaches you to control your strength; the self-control of God is how you choose the greater "YES."

How refreshing and attractive! All of this is one "fruit" that grows out of the time you spend with God each day. You don't have to try to do the right things to be loved. You're already loved by God, and His love will transform you into the kind of person who does the right things.

What is a next step you can take in letting God grow you? How will you trust Him in this? Take some time to jot your thoughts down on the opposite page.

ARE YOU TAKING YOUR VITAMINS?

Did you grow up taking a daily vitamin? Were they gummies? I bet they were. Maybe they still are…?

I didn't grow up taking vitamins. I'd like to say it was because I ate so many vegetables every day that I didn't need the vitamin supplement, but that wouldn't be true. I'm sure my mom tried to start the good habit early on and then just gave up when met with my annoying resistance. However, I'm happy to report, as an adult, I take a vitamin every day. Props to me!

If you didn't know, the concept for taking a daily vitamin is to be sure you receive the needed amounts of vitamin C, D, calcium, etc. each day. It turns out that I'm not the only one missing the mark on daily vegetable consumption. Someone way smarter than you and me figured out how much of everything we need and then packed it into a gummy.

Here's the crazy part: I have no idea how the vitamin actually does the good it's intended to do in my body. I don't understand the science of it all, but I take it anyway. Why? Because I know it's good for me and my health. So, even though I am clueless as to HOW it's improving my health, I trust that it is.

How do you think this could relate to your faith journey?

I'd like to offer three spiritual vitamins I'm convinced will do good, even produce goodness, in our lives if we take them regularly.

Spiritual Vitamin #1: God's Word

Has a youth pastor, parent, preacher, or grandma ever told you that you should read the Bible? Not just once or twice a year, but every day? Have you tried to do that?

I bet you have, and I'm going to guess it didn't last very long. Why? Because you seemingly didn't see any tangible value in the reading of your Bible. Your grades were still well below average. Your ex-boyfriend still ignored you. And your starting spot on the team was still taken by the new kid who showed up out of nowhere last fall.

But what if reading God's Word actually was doing something to influence your heart, mind, and soul, but you just didn't realize it?

Read the following verses and write your answer to this question for each: How could this truth influence your perspective, attitude, or mood if you read it and absorbed it?

"The Lord is near to the brokenhearted and saves the crushed in spirit." (Psalm 34:18)

Possible answer: The next time you're hurting because your ex-boyfriend is ignoring you, you might pray to God because you remember that you heard He is close to those who are hurting.

"'All things are lawful for me,' but not all things are helpful. 'All things are lawful for me,' but I will not be dominated by anything." (1 Corinthians 6:12)

The amazing part about God's incredible character is that, in the same moment, He is both powerful and personal. In the same moment, He is in charge of all that is happening around the globe, and He sees you and cares about the situation you're in.

If you're willing to trust that His Word is doing good in you, even if it doesn't seem like it, He will do good on your behalf.

The next time you're chewing that grape gummy vitamin, ask yourself, "Am I willing to do the same with God's Word?"

Spiritual Vitamin #2: Prayer

Just like you have been encouraged to read the Bible by well-meaning adults in your life, I'm sure you've been told to pray. Finding a way to pray that keeps you engaged and on track is tough, though! The TACO way seems to be the perfect answer for a teenager!

As you come to the Lord in prayer, use this rhythm:

- **T**hanks (for what He has done)
- **A**doration (for who He is)
- **C**onfession (for what you have done)
- **O**thers (what the people around you need)
- **S**elf (what you need)

In Jeremiah 33:3, God says, **"Call to Me and I will answer you, and will tell you great and hidden things that you have not known."** Let's take Him up on that by TACOing every day!

Spiritual Vitamin #3: Christian Community

We were not intended to live life alone. God said it Himself in Genesis 2:18. When we're isolated from others by force or choice, we're not living how God intended us to. Being created in the image of God means we have the desire to be in relationships infused into us.

"BEING CREATED IN THE IMAGE OF GOD MEANS WE HAVE THE DESIRE TO BE IN RELATIONSHIPS INFUSED INTO US."

Whether you consider yourself a people person or prefer your alone time, you know the gift of being seen, known, and loved by someone. It feels good. It feels right. That's because it's how we were designed!

The fun thing is that Christian community can take different forms—one-on-one discipling, small group, youth group, school Bible study, book club, bonfires at your youth leader's house, or even shopping for prom dresses with like-minded friends.

As you move into the rest of your day, answer this question: Which spiritual vitamin do you need a higher dose of in your life right now?

EXPERIENCE: 7 TESTS OF A HEALTHY DATING RELATIONSHIP

What's the purpose of dating in high school? It's surprising how many teenagers haven't thought through their philosophy of dating. They've thought through their plan to get their driver's license. They can articulate how completing certain AP courses will get them into prestigious colleges. They even have thoughtful support as to which NBA team or social media platform is the best. But ask them about their philosophy of dating, and you get a blank stare or a shrug of the shoulders.

As a teenager who professes faith in Christ, having a dating philosophy is important!

Don't try to figure this one out on your own! *Proverbs 15:22 says, "Without counsel plans fail, but with many advisers they succeed."* Grab a few wise people around you—peers and adults—treat them to some fro-yo and nail down your philosophy on dating. To get the wheels turning, you might want to start with questions like:

- What is the purpose of dating?
- What are the advantages and disadvantages of exclusive dating?
- What's the end game?
- What do my parents think about dating?
- What does the Bible say about male and female relationships?

No matter when you choose to date, one of the main goals of dating should be to have a healthy relationship. What better way to find out if you are in or ready for a healthy relationship than to take a quiz? Below are seven (fun!) tests of a healthy dating relationship. As you work through them, rate yourself on a scale of 1-5, 1 being "Wow, I've/we've got a long way to go!" and 5 being "I/We're not perfect, but solid."

1. The Puke Test | My score: _____

Everyone loves a good puke story, don't they? The little kid who overate on the mac-n-cheese, followed by three juice boxes. His chubby cheeks try to keep it in, but instead, it shoots out his mouth and hits the van window and the back of his mom's head as she drives.

Maybe you have an even better puke story that includes someone holding your hair back as you puke in the toilet or hard-shell tacos coming back up, not having been digested! The main question of the puke test is: Has the person seen you at your worst, physically, emotionally, or relationally? If the answer is "No," then you are not in a healthy relationship!

Real life is filled with puking, anxiety attacks, migraines, bad hair days, meltdowns, and irrational moments. If the person you are with has only seen you at your best and put together, then he/she has not seen all of you.

2. The Target Test | My score: _____

Physical attraction is a fun part of a relationship. When you wait for God's best and have sex when you are married, sex is also a fun part of the relationship. But, here's the truth—on a REALLY great week, sex makes up maybe 5% of a marriage! And that's on a really great week!

Do you know what the other 95% of marriage is? Going to Target. Mowing the lawn. Walking the dog. Paying bills. Grocery shopping. The main question for the Target Test is: Can you have fun doing everyday activities?

It doesn't matter how amazing your physical chemistry is; there's no way 5% of your relationship can make up for the rest of the 95%! If you are in a healthy relationship, you are laughing together as you attempt to make a birthday cake for your grandma. You're joking around as you stack chairs in the youth room. You're chilling on the back deck, reading.

3. The Friends & Family Test | My score: _____

Have you ever heard the phrase "blinded by love?" It means you are so into someone that you can only see the good and you ignore the bad. On the surface, it may seem like a sweet quality in a relationship, but it is definitely an indicator of an unhealthy relationship. A real relationship acknowledges the good and the bad, desiring an honest evaluation of the relationship. That's where the main question of the Friends & Family Test comes in: Do your family and friends approve of the person you are dating?

No one knows you better than your friends and family! They have been with you for the long haul and have proven their love for you. If you are in a healthy relationship, you have intentionally invited your friends and family to offer their perspectives. Are you open to their view and opinions? If you are, that points to you being in a healthy relationship.

Here's a life tip…if you find yourself being defensive when your friends and family point out flaws within your relationship, that's often a sign that you know, deep down, they're right. If their opinions were way out there, you would dismiss them and not feel the need to be defensive. Keep your response in check!

4. The Jesus Test | My score: _____

As someone who has said "Yes" to following Jesus, passing this test is a must. The Apostle Paul, in 2 Corinthians 6:14-16, warns Christians of being intimately connected with those who are not Christians: *"Do not be unequally yoked with unbelievers. For what partnership has righteousness with lawlessness? Or what fellowship has light with darkness? What accord has Christ with Belial? Or what portion does a believer share with an unbeliever? What agreement has the temple of God with idols? For we are the temple of the living God…"*

To be fair, this passage is referring to marriage, but the ultimate end game of dating, for a Christian, is marriage, right? The main question for the Jesus Test is: Are you dating a passionate follower of Jesus Christ? Notice the question is not "Are you dating a Christian?" There are too many soft definitions of what a Christian is in our world—someone who goes to church, was baptized as a baby, believes in God, or prays. Those are all good attributes, but a healthy relationship requires you to be with a passionate follower of Jesus!

5. The Pie Test | My score: _____

If you love pie, this test will make sense to you. Imagine that you and your special one are hanging out on the weekend and remember your mom made a peanut butter cup pie! You bolt upstairs to the kitchen and are relieved to find there are two slices left! Perfect!

As you are transferring the pie to the plates, you realize one slice is significantly larger than the other. Uh-oh. In that moment, you have a choice. And this is where the main question comes up for the Pie Test: Do you give or keep the bigger piece of pie? (Technically, there is another option—you eating from the sides of the bigger slice to make it the same size as the other, but we're working to be like Jesus here, okay?!)

In Philippians 2:3-4, Paul challenges us with these words, *"Do nothing from selfish ambition or conceit, but in humility count others more significant than yourselves. Let each of you look not only to his own interests, but also to the interests of others."*

If you are in a healthy relationship, you genuinely want the best for the other person. It brings you joy to see them get the bigger slice! Know what's even cooler? In a healthy relationship, they feel the same way about you getting the bigger slice!

6. The G-Time Test | My score: _____

A classic move in a teenage dating relationship is that the couple is attached at the hip. If they are in the same zip code, they are right next to each other, moving as one. Because they are all about each other, they separate themselves from everyone else. The guys he used to game with on the weekends are having to eat his share of the pizza and wings because he's a no-show. The girls she did shopping sprees with weekly are one short in their carpool to the mall.

The main question for the G-time Test is: Are you investing as much energy and time in your Guy/Girl-Time as you are in your dating relationship? It's unrealistic to ask one person to meet all your needs. No one but Jesus can do that! God made us for community, and we need to be in it! As a general guideline, if you spend Friday on a date, spend Saturday with your guys or your girls—50/50. If you do that, you can probably call yourself healthy!

7. The No Touch Test | My score: _____

This may be seen as the most controversial test of all! In a season of life when the hormones are running wild, the main question for the No Touch Test is: Can you go 30 days without touching each other? No kissing, holding hands, arms around each other, or hugging. Nothing. It's a tough but telling test.

1 Thessalonians 4:3-5, Paul tells us that we should be different if we call ourselves Christians: *"For this is the will of God, your sanctification: that you abstain from sexual immorality; that each one of you know how to control his own body in holiness and honor, not in the passion of lust like the Gentiles who do not know God..."*

It's hard and easy to be different when you're a Christian teenager. Hard because your natural tendency is to want to stay under the radar, go with the flow of culture. Easy because this world has turned from God and the simple act of controlling your own body will be seen as different.

Possible results of attempting the 30-Day No Touch Test:

* You won't make it past 48 hours! Conclusion: Your relationship is too focused on the physical.

* You make it, but you're completely bored with the other person. Conclusion: Your relationship is too focused on physical and/or you don't really like each other; you're just attracted to each other.

* You make it and feel more connected than you ever have been! Conclusion: Your relationship is not based on just the physical, but on the intimacy of conversation and spending time together.

My test total: _____

28-35: You are well on your way to being in a healthy relationship! Continue to pay attention to the right areas, and you will be better for it!

21-27: You have a decent base for a healthy relationship, but need to apply some laser focus to a couple areas. Choose one this week to tackle and enjoy the healthy results!

UNDER 20: If you are currently in a relationship, you should have some serious conversations. This is the time in your life to work on you! Ask the Lord to show you what areas you should lean into, with His help, and then do it! Surround yourself with people who are for you, and have fun becoming healthy!

HOW MUCH CAN I SPEND ON SHOES?

How is your shoe game? Are you wearing the latest Jordans with plenty of back-ups in the closet? Selling sneakers and making money? Or are you happy just to have a new pair of Crocs? No matter how you would rate your shoe game, you are well aware of our society's focus on the external. Shoes. Fashion. Your flow. Waist lines. Muscle tone.

It's interesting that much of Scripture acknowledges the physical—whether or not someone is handsome, beautiful, or plain—but focuses on the importance of character. One of the places we see this is when we are introduced to David. You might remember the story—the prophet Samuel is sent by God to anoint the King of Israel. King Saul, who was a strong and handsome man, wasn't living up to the standard, and God wanted to choose a special man to lead His special people, the Israelites.

Samuel comes to the home of Jesse in Bethlehem to anoint the new king. Jesse had a lot of sons, and physically, they were impressive. Big. Chiseled. Probably with strong jawlines. Seven of them passed in front of Samuel, but God did not choose any of them. In 1 Samuel 16:7, we see God's declaration to Samuel: *"Do not look on his appearance or on the height of his stature, because I have rejected him. For the Lord sees not as man sees: man looks on the outward appearance, but the Lord looks on the heart."*

When David stood in front of Samuel, God said, "Arise, anoint him, for this is he." The Bible says David was very handsome, but there was so much more below that rugged exterior.

David was far from perfect, but he's later called a man after God's own heart. That's special. He loved and sought after the Lord, showing the importance of internal character and strength. So, how is your heart game?

In the New Testament, the apostle Peter makes a similar claim, this time specifically for the ladies. 1 Peter 3:3-4 says, *"Do not let your adorning be external—the braiding of hair and the putting on of gold jewelry, or the clothing you wear—but let your adorning be the hidden person of the heart with the imperishable beauty of a gentle and quiet spirit, which in God's sight is very precious."*

Isn't it fascinating that thousands of years ago, the temptation was strong to get attention and value from what was on the outside? Sounds like it's a human condition, not just a modern-day issue.

Notice that Peter doesn't say you can't look good or accessorize. It says your beauty should not come from the outside. It's tricky, though, isn't it? Because when you look good, people notice and say something about it. That feels good. So, you wear that outfit again. You work those biceps a little more. And people notice. The cycle goes on and on. But that's the problem. That cycle never ends. The difficult part is not letting your outward appearance become more important than your character.

How's your heart game? How much are you willing to pay for solid character?

Choose one of these three takeaway options and commit to following through on it:

1. In your own handwriting, put the verses above on a notecard. (You're not using those notecards for studying anyway!) Post that notecard somewhere you'll see it every day. On the bath room mirror. Above your light switch. On the dash of your car.

2. One day this week, track how much time you spend on your external (showering, dressing, make-up, working out, etc.) and block out the same amount of time to spend investing in your internal (reading the Bible, doing a devo, talking with a friend about what you're both learning from God).

3. Identify an adult in your world who is of strong, godly character and also happens to be physically attractive. Share the highlighted verses with them and ask how they keep their focus on the internal versus the external. Take notes and put them into practice!

WHAT DO YOU GET TO DO?

Have you ever been into puzzles? If so, what was your ideal number of pieces to try to solve? Twenty? Fifty? One hundred? One thousand? This is obvious, but the more pieces there are, the longer it takes to assemble the puzzle.

Let's use that as an analogy for how each of us is made up of several different "pieces."

- When we're little, our pieces don't feel as numerous or complex. It's easy to find things in common with others and make friends for the easiest of reasons. *"Oh, you like grape soda? Me, too. Wanna come over to my house after school?"*

- The tween years are when some of those bigger pieces seem to get cut in half overnight. They sort of look the same, but now there are twice as many, and the picture on the box has more colors on it. It's like someone took markers and started doodling on it.

- When you become a teenager, you realize there are way more pieces to who you are than you ever thought possible. Someone also apparently ripped off the cover of the box, so you're not sure what your reference is for what you're supposed to do. To survive, you pick a corner or two to try to make sense out of a few pieces while everyone older than you asks, "So, what will your completed puzzle look like when you graduate?"

- As you enter your young adult years, you can't even find the box anymore. It feels like you may have lost some essential pieces along the way, and you wonder if you'll ever get them back. Strangely, you do occasionally discover in your pockets some of those bigger pieces from when you were a kid.

> "SINGLENESS ISN'T ABOUT PURGING YOURSELF OF ANY DESIRE TO BE MARRIED. IT'S ABOUT DESIRING TO BE IN A RELATIONSHIP WITH GOD FIRST AND FOREMOST."

- By the time you're simply an "adult," you'll realize that it's not so much about every piece of your life fitting to complete the perfect puzzle but more about the relationships you build with others in helping each other simply place another piece. If someone's piece gets chewed up or broken, you bust out the tape and smooth it out. You start to become just as interested in helping them form their puzzles as you are in building your own.

- Should you become a senior citizen, well, that's just amazing. You spend your years deciding if it's time to show off all the puzzles you've completed or (even better) invest in the puzzles of the next generation.

Now, that could be your timeline. You could live life simply focused on pursuing everything and everyone who might somehow "complete" you. It might take you until adulthood to realize this is the wrong approach. Some adults, in fact, still need to learn this. Real hope isn't found in striving to put down another piece in your puzzle but in the work of God piecing you together.

So... what do you get to do? You get to let Him do this in you and help Him do this in others.

"Let us hold fast the confession of our hope without wavering, for He who promised is faithful. And let us consider how to stir up one another to love and good works, not neglecting to meet together, as is the habit of some, but encouraging one another, and all the more as you see the Day drawing near." (Hebrews 10:23-25)

That's right – you get to spur others on as God builds you up.

Sure, you have a lot of puzzle pieces to sort through in life. You always will. Only in Heaven are we finally "perfected" by God. Why not let Him start that even now?

SINGLENESS ISN'T ABOUT PURGING YOURSELF OF ANY DESIRE TO BE MARRIED.
It's about desiring to be in a relationship with God first and foremost. Write out a prayer to Him here, whether you're currently single or not, sharing in detail how this is your heart's desire.

DATING ISN'T JUST A PATHWAY TO GET MARRIED. It's a pathway for kindness. Think about how you've either dated with self-interest or seen others date that way. Again, write out a prayer here that any dating you do or see others do will be an opportunity to see and experience kindness throughout the relationship that leads toward love and good deeds.

FRIENDSHIP ISN'T ABOUT FINDING PEOPLE TO VENT TO. IT'S ABOUT FINDING PEOPLE WHO NEED TO FEEL THE FRESH BREATH OF THE LORD UPON THEM THROUGH YOU. Think about your friend circle. Who seems to be worn down or could use some encouragement, if not even an arm around their shoulder? Write down three names here.

1.

2.

3.

ROMANCE ISN'T ABOUT A DRAMATIC EXPRESSION THAT ENSNARES SOMEONE. It's about a creative expression that cares for someone. Decide how you'll help everyone in your circle see it this way – that shady flirting is sketchy all over, but the best kind of romance lets someone else realize they're special. Maybe help each other get better at this by brainstorming creative ideas in a book that anyone can use and call upon the help of friends to do. Write down two ideas here.

How will you spur one another on toward love and good deeds?

WHY ARE YOU "IN LIKE" ANYWAY?

Have you ever thought about the difference between friendship with someone and dating them? It might surprise you, but there's not much of a difference.

Think about it. Anything you do while dating can be done with a friend…except for the physical. That's the only distinguishing factor. You can laugh, eat, play video games, workout, shoot each other with Nerf guns, listen to music, swim, do a Bible study, cook, go to the dog park, knit, and ride roller coasters.

Just to solidify the point, add six other activities you can do with non-dating friends:

1.

2.

3.

4.

5.

6.

"SEX WAS CREATED BY GOD, AND EVEN THOUGH IT'S NATURAL AND INTENDED, HE GIVES US BOUNDARIES SO WE CAN ENJOY THE PHYSICAL RELATIONSHIP TO ITS FULLEST WHEN THE TIME IS RIGHT"

You know this—many Christian teenagers are so determined to claim the status of being a couple that they don't think things through! In their excitement, they ignore the fact that sexual temptation is one of Satan's greatest tools to use against Christians. In classic Satan form, he takes something that was created by God for His glory and our good, and he warps it.

We were created to be sexual beings. Touch is meant to excite us. That shock that goes up your arm when he holds your hand? Intended by God. The heat you feel under your skin when she grabs your leg during the scary part of the movie? Fashioned by God.

Sex was created by God, and even though it's natural and intended, He gives us boundaries so we can enjoy the physical relationship to its fullest when the time is right.

How many young adults have proclaimed, "I won't have sex until I'm married," one of the most counter-cultural choices you can make, and yet have no idea where to find that command in the Bible? God's call for us to be holy is laced throughout the Bible, but here are two big ones when it comes to sexual holiness:

"Let marriage be held in honor among all, and let the marriage bed be un-defiled, for God will judge the sexually immoral and adulterous." (Hebrews 13:4)

"For this is the will of God, your sanctification: that you abstain from sexual immorality; that each one of you know how to control his own body in holiness and honor, not in the passion of lust like the Gentiles who do not know God; that no one transgress and wrong his brother in this matter, because the Lord is an avenger in all these things, as we told you before-hand and solemnly warned you. For God has not called us for impurity, but in holiness." (1 Thessalonians 4:3-7)

How cool is it that God cares about how you express yourself sexually?

If you have committed your life to Jesus, you are supposed to be different, set apart from others, and abide by God's design for sexuality. That's the main message of the verses above. This feels like a big ask to a teenager who mostly just wants to fit in and stay under the radar. And yet, God has been asking this of His people since He had His people. Being set apart is for God's glory and our good.

How about a different view on dating? Or a different take on opposite-gender friendship? Instead of spending significant time dating one person and fighting to control your own body in holiness and honor, why not invest in "liking?"

Ways to invest in "liking:"
- Learn what it's like to like who God created you to be.
- Hang out with people of the opposite gender in groups to learn what qualities you like in others.
- If your parents are cool with it, spend some one-on-one time with someone you like. Don't get sucked into a physical relationship, just do fun activities together.

You might be surprised how much fun liking someone can be! And how uncomplicated that relationship can be without the physical aspect!

What kind of freedom do you think can come from just investing in "liking" without feeling the need to be dating?

DO YOU KNOW WHAT YOU'RE DOING?

What do you do each day without even knowing it? Do you bite your fingernails? Play with your hair? Bounce your leg up and down in class? Stare into space? All of us do things involuntarily or without thought.

But there are plenty of actions we take with full knowledge! We annoy our siblings. Ignore our chores. Lie about the status of our work. Throw trash on the ground. Walk right by the pile our dog left in the backyard. Most of the time, we are well aware of what we're doing.

When it comes to relationships with the opposite gender, do you know what you're doing?

> "WITH THE SPIRIT OF GOD LIVING INSIDE YOU, LIFE CAN BE AND SHOULD BE DIFFERENT— A HOLY KIND OF DIFFERENT."

Here's a quick check-in. Circle one of the options in each pairing and write at least two sentences in the space provided to support your answer.

ARE YOU...

Building up or tearing down?

Treating with respect or disrespect?

Sending clear or mixed messages?

What you do, with thought or without thought, matters. How you speak. The look you give. The way you dress. What you look at online. The text you send. The picture you Snap. It all matters in your relationships with others.

The Apostle Paul spent a good amount of time helping the early Christians learn how to live together. Following Jesus as a group was a new deal, and people came from different ways of life. Sometimes, tension was an inevitable reality. This was certainly the case for the church at Colossae. Here is an excerpt of what Paul wrote to them in Colossians 3:12-14:

COMPASSIONATE HEARTS, KINDNESS, HUMILITY, MEEKNESS, PATIENCE, BEARING WITH ONE ANOTHER, FORGIVENESS, AND LOVE.

"Put on then, as God's chosen ones, holy and beloved, compassionate hearts, kindness, humility, meekness, and patience, bearing with one another and, if one has a complaint against another, forgiving each other; as the Lord has forgiven you, so you also must forgive. And above all these put on love, which binds everything together in perfect harmony."

If you were to use Paul's instructions in these verses as your gauge, how would you score yourself on how you treat the opposite sex? Circle or highlight the eight qualities noted in the Scripture verses above. Then, rank them below, 1-8, with #1 being your strongest quality and #8 being your most lacking quality.

1.

2.

3.

4.

5.

6.

7.

8.

In the culture you're growing up in, it seems like anything goes. You be you. Live your truth. Follow your heart. Do what you need to do. Take care of yourself. These statements are almost the exact opposite of the spirit of Paul's writing. It's as if we're called to be different than the world we're living in…huh…(*sips tea*)

You are capable of so much more than this world gives you credit for! Especially when it comes to how you interact with and treat the opposite sex. Don't believe the lie that you "can't help it" or "boys will be boys!" With the Spirit of God living inside you, life can be and should be different—a holy kind of different.

In the next week, use Colossians 3:12-14 as your daily prayer. Start your day (maybe even in front of your mirror!) saying these words out loud and asking God to help you live them out. Then, go into your world with the intention of knowing exactly what you're doing—treating others like God treats you!

"PUT ON THEN, AS GOD'S CHOSEN ONES, HOLY AND BELOVED, COMPASSIONATE HEARTS, KINDNESS, HUMILITY, MEEKNESS, AND PATIENCE, BEARING WITH ONE ANOTHER AND, IF ONE HAS A COMPLAINT AGAINST ANOTHER, FORGIVING EACH OTHER; AS THE LORD HAS FORGIVEN YOU, SO YOU ALSO MUST FORGIVE. AND ABOVE ALL THESE PUT ON LOVE, WHICH BINDS EVERYTHING TOGETHER IN PERFECT HARMONY."

WHAT ARE YOU STUFFING YOURSELF WITH?

Have you ever taken a punch in the face? Probably not in the ring like a title fighter, but maybe an emotional punch? A relational punch in the gut that takes your breath away? Let's be honest, sometimes life can feel like a fight, 12 full rounds! Your days are spent bobbing and weaving to avoid punches and throwing punches of protection yourself.

Even if you can't claim to be an expert on boxing or UFC fighting, you're smart enough to know that what happens outside the ring significantly affects what happens in the ring. The fighter's workout regimen. Her diet. His coaching. Her water intake. All of it matters when they step in the ring for a fight.

If life is like a fight in the ring, what are you doing to prepare yourself for the fight? The first step in preparing for a fight is knowing who you're up against, so check out what Ephesians 6:12 says about our opponent: ***"For we do not wrestle against flesh and blood, but against the rulers, against the authorities, against the cosmic powers over this present darkness, against the spiritual forces of evil in the heavenly places."***

The Apostle Paul talks about the importance of preparing for the fight in chapter 5 of his letter to the Galatians. Those in the church of Galatia were new Christians attempting to live together in Christian community. As they related to one another, they often found the old versions of themselves coming to the surface and causing issues. Look at how Paul explained the choice they have every day:

"But I say, walk by the Spirit, and you will not gratify the desires of the flesh. For the desires of the flesh are against the Spirit, and the desires of the Spirit are against the flesh, for these are opposed to each other, to keep you from doing the things you want to do. But if you are led by the Spirit, you are not under the law.

Now the works of the flesh are evident: sexual immorality, impurity, sensuality, idolatry, sorcery, enmity, strife, jealousy, fits of anger, rivalries, dissensions, divisions, envy, drunkenness, orgies, and things like these. I warn you, as I warned you before, that those who do such things will not inherit the kingdom of God. But the fruit of the Spirit is love, joy, peace, patience, kindness, goodness, faithfulness, gentleness, self-control; against such things there is no law.

And those who belong to Christ Jesus have crucified the flesh with its pas-sions and desires. If we live by the Spirit, let us also keep in step with the Spirit. Let us not become conceited, provoking one another, envying one another." (Galatians 5:16-26)

That's a lot, but here's a quick summary: Every day, you have a choice to feed the Spirit that lives inside you or to feed your own flesh. Your choice will directly affect your prepa-ration and your fight. So, what are you stuffing yourself with? If you feed the Spirit, good will win. If you feed your flesh, evil will win. Go back and circle the examples of good and the examples of evil that Paul lists in the passage above.

One list sure is more attractive than the other, isn't it?

You might be wondering, "What does 'feeding' mean? Are we talking about choosing asparagus over Doritos? Apples over Airheads?" That's a fair question.

When we say feeding, we're talking about which desires you're submitting to. Are you submitting to the Spirit's desires? Or are you submitting to your own fleshly desires? It comes down to what you're allowing into your body—through your eyes, your ears, and, yes, maybe even your mouth! Each time you pick up your phone, choose a playlist, start a show, follow an influencer, twist off a cap, go to a website, or read a book, you are choos-ing to either submit to the Spirit of God in you or your own fleshly desires. What you look at, listen to, watch, follow, drink, or read is either pulling you toward God or pushing you away from God. There is no neutral.

In verse 17, Paul writes, **"For the desires of the flesh are against the Spirit, and the desires of the Spirit are against the flesh, for these are opposed to each other, to keep you from doing the things you want to do."** Take a few minutes to make this real for you.

How do you experience this fight in your own life? (Example: You really want to honor your parents, but it's hard when they ask you to take out the garbage when you're in the middle of an online game that you can't just pause.)

WHAT'S THE PENALTY?

Ever gotten in trouble or known someone who's gotten into trouble for doing one thing wrong?

"But it was just that one time."

That's the defense, isn't it? Parents, teachers, bosses, coaches, and pastors have all heard it. Maybe you have, too.

"YOU'RE GROUNDED FROM USING YOUR PHONE FOR A WEEK AFTER BEING RECKLESS WITH IT."

"But it was just that one time."

"You didn't feed the dog all day, so to help you remember he exists, you get to scoop up after him in the yard right now and give him a bath each week for the next four weeks."

"But it was just that one time."

Not to be too candid, but your doctor probably hears this, too. Physicians have the unique job of evaluating their patients and saying what they see, whether or not it's surprising.

"GUESS WHAT? YOU'RE PREGNANT."

"But it was just that one time."

"THAT'S ALL IT TAKES."

Remember all of that as we talk about the word "penalty" in the world of relationships. You may believe the worst thing that can happen if you cross a line is that someone else holds you accountable for it.

King David wrestled with this by having a life in the public eye. He grew up loving the Lord and eventually became a fierce warrior and God-honoring ruler. But his actions didn't always line up with this.

David, unfortunately, started making decisions outside of God's will. He married multiple women, had concubines, and even faded back from the job of leading his army into battle. One night, while on a rooftop, he saw a beautiful woman taking a bath and used his position as king to have her brought to him for one night of sex that crossed all kinds of lines (especially since she was already married…to a man that was not David). She ended up pregnant.

"But it was just that one time."

"THAT'S ALL IT TAKES."

David tried to get her actual husband, Uriah, to have sex with her, so maybe he'd assume he got her pregnant. When that didn't work, David went further down the black hole of sin. He arranged for Uriah to die on the battlefield, and then David gave all the appearances of being a righteous man by marrying the widow Bathsheba. Yep, he murdered a man to cover up his other sin.

"But it was just that one time."

"THAT'S ALL IT TAKES."

God revealed all this to a prophet named Nathan, who confronted David even though he knew David had the power to murder him to keep the cover-up going. Instead, David listened to all of the consequences that would happen from what he did – how his family would become that much more violent and sexually scandalous. David owned his sin, and the prophet added that God forgave him, but there was still one more consequence – the child inside of Bathsheba would die.

"But it was just that one time."

"THAT'S ALL IT TAKES."

In light of all of that, do you really think the worst thing that could happen if you disregard God and sin as you please is that someone else will hold you accountable for it?

What about the guilt you walk around with? Damaged relationships? Shame from other people knowing? Emotional anxiety? Inner conflict? Tangible impact on life and death? Loss of community? Impact on future relationships? Disconnect from God? Deterioration of values?

Yes, all of that is possible. Still, that may not be the worst thing that could happen to you. For a clue on that, look at the introduction to Psalm 51:

"To the choirmaster. A Psalm of David, when Nathan the prophet went to him, after he had gone in to Bathsheba."

What follows are moments of prayer like, *"For I know my transgressions, and my sin is ever before me"* and *"Create in me a clean heart, O God, and renew a right spirit within me." (Psalm 51:3, 10)*

Are you catching what David is saying? "God, I can't deny my sin. I'm looking at it, and I finally see it for what it is. It's so bad inside me that I want You to create a clean heart in me because mine is filthy."

The penalty for not trusting God, rejecting His commands, and ignoring His wisdom is that one day, judgment is coming. You can keep living in sin for a long time and maybe feel better about it by using your favorite excuse. You might even get really good at putting others in their place when they challenge you.

At some point, though, you will have to bend your knee to God and see, face-to-face, just how dark things have gotten. You'll either choose to do this on Earth or fall flat on your face when you stand before a holy God after death.

So David, whose heart had strayed, decided to go after God's heart again. Not only did he do the hard and ugly work of staring at his sin and owning it, but he made his sin public. Psalm 51 isn't a private journal, but something he set to music…so his sin would be a memorable object lesson for everyone. Can you imagine doing that with your sinful choices?

Now…what lines have you been crossing and excusing? Which ones would you easily cross if given the chance? Are you going to keep going after all of that privately, hoping not to get caught and excusing it if you do? Or are you so willing to avoid sin and all its decay that you'll go public with others about what's really happening? More importantly, will you bring it to God and confess that you've wandered away?

Even one simple conversation with the right person can get you growing again. You might even look back on that conversation fondly, surprised that it ignited a transformation in you.

What do you need to confess to God? What excuses do you need to give up and lay at the feet of Jesus?

More importantly, what are you waiting on? God is listening.

One of the biggest lies infiltrating the church is that desiring anyone outside of marriage is okay as long as we don't act on those desires. When you're asked, "Who do you like?", "Who's your crush?" or "Which celebrity do you think is hot?", we often think these conversations are harmless because we're not sinning outwardly. However, sin starts in the heart. James 1:13-15 explains that sin begins with our desires. The moment we start desiring things that go against God's will, like desiring people we're not married to, sin takes root. Instead of engaging in 'harmless' conversations about our inward fallen desires, we should flee from them and ask God to change our hearts.
- Harrison, 26

DO YOU TRUST GOD WITH YOUR CRUSH?

You see him in the lunch room and almost drop that slice of pizza in your lap. You see her in the soprano section and can't read your tenor part right in front of you. You get dizzy. You can't speak. You feel like you're falling over yourself. You walk straight into the glass door.

You're crushing. Hard.

Does God care? As He's, you know, running the whole universe, does He care about how much you want to be with this person? Does He hear your prayers? Does He want this longing inside you to be fulfilled? Yes, He does! And He knows the best He has in store for you.

Here's the truth: If it's God's will for you to be in a romantic, exclusive relationship with your crush, there's nothing you can do to stop it.

How's that for confidence? How's that for assurance? Support for this truth is all throughout Scripture, but here are two verses that highlight the unstoppable nature of God's will:

"The counsel of the Lord stands forever, the plans of His heart to all generations." (Psalm 33:11)

"Many are the plans in the mind of a man, but it is the purpose of the Lord that will stand." (Proverbs 19:21)

Take a moment to write your thoughts in response to these verses about trusting Him with your crush (look for the words or phrases that communicate the confidence you can have in God):

When we have a crush, we often take matters into our own hands. We attempt to control, not trust. We try to manipulate, not obey. Rather than trying to make things happen ourselves, why not follow David's instruction in Psalm 37:3-4? ***"Trust in the Lord, and do good; dwell in the land and befriend faithfulness. Delight yourself in the Lord, and He will give you the desires of your heart."***

What does THAT look like?

Rather than spending all your energy trying to get your crush to realize you're the perfect match, how about rerouting that energy to "trust in the Lord and do good?" Instead of obsessing over their social media, why not volunteer in the children's ministry at your church? Instead of shoving friends out of the way to sit by your crush at youth group, why not sit by the student who came by himself for the first time? Instead of staring off into space with dreams of the two of you together, why not open your Bible and fill that space with God's truth? That's doing good while trusting God.

How about taking it a step further to "dwell in the land and befriend faithfulness?" As a shepherd, David often used shepherding terms and ideas to describe God and our relationship with Him. The shepherd's primary responsibility is the care and protection of his sheep. His sheep are in the safest place when they are in the land meant for them. There, the shepherd can keep a close watch on them. Right now, when you are dwelling with God, you are right where He wants you to be. Relax. Enjoy. He's got you.

"IF IT'S GOD'S WILL FOR YOU TO BE IN A ROMANTIC, EXCLUSIVE RELATIONSHIP WITH YOUR CRUSH, THERE'S NOTHING YOU CAN DO TO STOP IT."

Although it's true that you can't stop God's will if He wants you with your crush, it's important to remember this: Those who have said "Yes!" to Jesus ultimately pray for God's will to be done, even if it's not what they would prefer. It's okay, and even healthy, to let the Lord know what our desires are (He knows them anyway! See Psalm 139:4), but we always need to come back to "Not my will, but Your will be done."

As you think about your crush today, can you say that? Are you willing to accept God's will, even if it's not what you want it to be?

EXPERIENCE: WHO'S THE G.O.A.T.?

Among all of the possible things someone could be good at, just think about the numerous people across different fields who are thought to be the Greatest Of All Time.

Michael Jordan is widely regarded as the greatest basketball player of all time, with an impact on the sport that's unparalleled. Serena Williams is thought to be one of the most dominant tennis players in history, redefining the sport with her unmatched skill and determination. Usain Bolt is known as the fastest man in the world and has legendary sprinting prowess. Leonardo da Vinci is the original "Renaissance Man" who excelled in painting, sculpture, science, engineering, and anatomy. Marie Curie was a pioneering physicist and chemist who won Nobel Prizes in two different scientific fields (Physics and Chemistry) for her groundbreaking research that laid the foundation for modern nuclear physics. Muhammad Ali is revered as recreating what people might expect of a boxer, from his charisma, athleticism, and social activism.

Who's the G.O.A.T. in the Bible when it comes to the topics we've been learning about?

If you couldn't say Jesus because…you know…He's always the right answer…who else would you pick? Who was nailing it socially? Who did well with the opposite gender? Who do you see standing on their own before they changed their relationship status? Who knew how to do romance well?

If that's the criteria, we're going to go with Solomon.

- **SINGLENESS:** When God offered him anything, he asked for wisdom. God gave it to him and blessed him with a lot of other extra blessings, too.
- **DATING:** The dude had 700 wives and 300 concubines. The Bible describes this, but God does not prescribe it (see Deuteronomy 17:17). From a cultural perspective alone, Solomon got around.
- **FRIENDSHIP:** He's described as attracting all kinds of people from all over the known world who came to spend time with him and listen to his wisdom. He freely gave them his time to help them sort out their needs.
- **ROMANCE:** There's a book in the Bible called "Song of Songs" (or "Song of Solomon") that shows the man knew how to woo a woman. We'll cover it a bit more later, but it's all poetic and has made lots of readers blush.

Ready for the big surprise?

After decades of living this way, he put this together:

"And whatever my eyes desired I did not keep from them. I kept my heart from no pleasure, for my heart found pleasure in all my toil, and this was my reward for all my toil. Then I considered all that my hands had done and the toil I had expended doing it, and behold, all was vanity and a striving after wind, and there was nothing to be gained under the sun."
(Ecclesiastes 2:10–11)

There you have it, from the alleged GOAT himself. He would have won awards in all four categories according to his culture, but it made him empty and angry on the inside. So many of his wives turned his heart away from God, too – but that didn't click for him until his later years.

If Solomon, who had wisdom from God and didn't always use it, wasn't confident in what he spent years doing, how confident are you in applying what we've been learning?

Now, let's put it to the test. After you read each prompt, invite God to help you write out a genuine response.

SINGLENESS

How do you view singleness? Why?

What should a single person spend his or her free time on? Why?

If you are/were single, what would be your greatest joy and your biggest struggle? Why?

DATING

In what areas of dating do you (or would you) drag your feet, and in what areas do you (or would you) tend to rush things? Why?

How would you specifically prioritize God in a dating relationship? Why?

What would healthy emotional boundaries, physical boundaries, and spiritual boundaries look like in a dating relationship you might be in? Why?

FRIENDSHIP

What kind of friend are you when it comes to regularly reaching out to your friends to check on how they're doing? Why?

Who is in your outer circle who could be an incredible part of your inner circle? Why?

What is a change you can make in how you're handling disappointment or conflict with a friend? Why?

ROMANCE

What do you believe should be true of every Christ-follower when it comes to romance? Why?

What is the purpose of romance? Why?

Describe the kind of romance you'd hope would be true of your marriage if you got married someday. Why?

As you're processing this, take note of what surprised or intrigued you as you wrote out your answers. It's not about being the Greatest Of All Time, but following the Greatest Of All Time.

Yes, that's Jesus…because…you know…He's always the right answer.

God created it, after all. What could you learn from Him about these things…

- Singleness, through how He uses his uniqueness to serve us: *"I am the Lord, and there is no other, besides Me there is no God; I equip you, though you do not know Me, that people may know, from the rising of the sun and from the west, that there is none besides me; I am the Lord, and there* is no other." (Isaiah 45:5-6)

- Dating, through how He lets us attach ourselves to Him: **"Take My yoke upon you, and learn from Me, for I am gentle and lowly in heart, and you will find rest for your souls."** (Matthew 11:29)

- Friendship, through how He comes to live inside of us: **"But the Helper, the Holy Spirit, whom the Father will send in My name, He will teach you all things and bring to your remembrance all that I have said to you."** (John 14:26)

- Romance, through His unique pursuit of His people: **"Therefore, behold, I will allure her, and bring her into the wilderness, and speak tenderly to her. And there I will give her her vineyards and make the Valley of Achor a door of hope. And there she shall answer as in the days of her youth, as at the time when she came out of the land of Egypt. And in that day, declares the Lord, you will call me 'My Husband,' and no longer will you call me 'My Baal.'"** (Hosea 2:14-16)

WHO'S TELLING YOU WHAT "WINNING" LOOKS LIKE?

It might help you to take a lesson from "Calvin Ball."

It comes from "Calvin & Hobbes" – one of the greatest comic strips ever that hits on friendship, family, school, bullies, and guy/girl attraction – all through the perspective of an imaginative boy with a wild streak, and his wise-yet-sarcastic stuffed tiger who comes to life in the boy's imagination.

So what are the rules of "Calvin Ball?" They're always changing! The game is all about making up new ways to play, all on the fly. You might be chasing a beach ball while hopping on one foot until someone says you now need to do it all backward while wearing a blindfold. The only consistent rule is that you can't play it the same way twice. It's all about keeping things fresh and unpredictable.

Who's telling you what winning looks like when it comes to singleness, dating, friendship, and romance?

You might say, "Well, you are! That's why I'm reading this book. I need to hear the instructions of incredible authors with wisdom that oozes out of them like hot queso drips onto nachos. Since you know everything on these topics, you can help me fix everything wrong in my life."

> "ON ONE HAND, GOD WANTS US TO NOT LISTEN TO THE ADVICE OF PEOPLE WHO ARE OUT OF STEP WITH HIM AND WITH US. ON THE OTHER HAND, HE DOES INVITE US TO HEAR HIM THROUGH A COMMUNITY OF PEOPLE AROUND US WHO FOLLOW HIM."

Well, shucks. You didn't have to lay it on so thick. Thank you for that sincere compliment. The reality is if we have any wisdom to offer you, we've been trying to use it to not just give you answers, but help you ask God better questions for all the "answers" you've been given.

So let's try it again – who's telling you what winning looks like when it comes to singleness, dating, friendship, and romance? Like Calvin Ball, it can feel like everyone around you is making up rules you're supposed to follow:

SINGLE? *"You shouldn't mind it." "You should totally mind it." "Keep your standards!" "Lower your standards!" "Stay where you are." "Go everywhere else." "Maybe God's going to surprise you."*

"Maybe you need to surprise God." "This is a blessing. The Bible says it's good to be single." "This is temporary. The Bible says to be fruitful and multiply."

- **DATING?** *"Are you doing a Bible study together?" "Do you study the Bible separately from each other?" "Only date if it's for marriage." "Don't worry about marriage yet." "Define everything." "Don't define everything." "You need accountability together." "You need accountability with others." "It doesn't matter what they believe." "It totally matters what they believe!"*

- **FRIENDSHIP?** *"Be friends with Christians who grow your faith." "Be friends with not-yet-Christians who need Jesus." "Give friends a big voice in your life." "Don't let friends be a big voice in your life." "Ignore drama to keep your friends." "Confront any awkward stuff as a caring friend." "Friendships change. Don't get attached." "Friendships can last. Go all in on them."*

- **ROMANCE?** *"It's up to the guy to say he's interested." "It's up to the girl to say she's interested." "Every anniversary is important – one week, one month, two months." "Relationships don't have to be so intense." "I think kissing/more/etc. is fine with anyone you want to do it with." "Don't be foolish by kissing/more/etc. someone you're into today but may not be with the rest of your life." "You should have matching t-shirts!" "If you wear matching t-shirts, we can no longer be friends."*

Which rules have you heard that you kind of agree with? Circle them above, and write one or two others down here:

Also, notice that the main question we first asked you isn't "What does winning look like," but "Who is telling you what it looks like?" That's the real question, isn't it?
There is a great, beautiful tension on this in the Bible:

"Blessed is the man who walks not in the counsel of the wicked, nor stands in the way of sinners, nor sits in the seat of scoffers..." (Psalm 1:1)

"Without counsel plans fail, but with many advisers they succeed." (Proverbs 15:22)

On one hand, God wants us to not listen to the advice of people who are out of step with Him and with us. On the other hand, He does invite us to hear Him through a community of people around us who follow Him. So when it comes to who is telling you things…

IS THIS SOMEONE WHO FOLLOWS GOD? You can get partially decent wisdom on anything from people who don't know God, as well as those who say they believe in

Him but pick and choose what they actually live out. When someone truly follows God themselves, though, they're less likely to steer you away from Him. If He's the ultimate first relationship in their lives, what impact could that have on you keeping Him first in everything in your life? **"Be imitators of me, as I am of Christ." (1 Cor. 11:1)**

IS THIS SOMEONE WHO LOVES YOU? The best kind of doctor doesn't tell you what makes you feel happy, but what makes you healthy – even if it doesn't make you happy. What if that's what the best kind of friend or family member does, too? Sure, they're great to do the most amazing things in the world with. What if they also were willing to point out your great decisions and show you your blind spots – not to criticize, but to help you grow? **"Faithful are the wounds of a friend; profuse are the kisses of an enemy." (Prov 27:6)**

IS THIS SOMEONE WHO UNDERSTANDS YOU? Anyone who doesn't know or like you can say something true-ish that makes you think, "Hmm. That sounded sort of accurate. Maybe I should listen to all of what this person says." Hang on…are you sure? Has that person taken the time to let you share your heart so they can grasp what's going on inside of you? If not, they may be offering quick advice out of their own regrets, insecurities, or experiences that you don't have to assume are true of your life. That's like them handing you their favorite hammer when you need a screwdriver. **"A fool takes no pleasure in understanding, but only in expressing his opinion." (Prov 18:2)**

IS THIS SOMEONE WHO TRUSTS YOU? Many people around you will offer advice they'd like to see you do right away. They may mean well and don't want you to waste your life. There comes a point when two-sided trust has to kick in, too. Ask for it by saying, "This is helpful. Thank you. I'm going to spend the next several days praying about how God might want me to take my first step. Trust me to keep you in the loop on how it goes, and I trust you to give me some space to figure this out on whatever timeline He shows me. Let's check in with each other soon. I'll let you know, okay?" In this way, you balance seeking wisdom while also letting God speak to you to sort out what to do. **"Ponder the path of your feet…Does not wisdom call? Does not understanding raise her voice?" (Proverbs 4:26a, 8:1)**

In the end, do you consider God as the One who actually does all of this? He is consistent, loves you, understands you, and trusts you! He can even use flawed people to remind you of His perfect wisdom, whether they directly say it or try to point you in the opposite direction.

What if you asked HIM to tell you what winning looks like?

☐ Yes, of course! God is God and I'm not. ☐ Maybe, I need to decide to trust God first.

WHAT ARE SOME "BEST FRIEND" DATES?

Is it possible to "just be friends" after breaking up with someone? That depends on whether you were actually ever friends before you started dating! How can you go back to something you don't know how to be?

That's why friendship with the opposite gender is such a great experience! Remember what was said in the "Why are you 'in like' anyway?" chapter? The only activity friendship doesn't promote is sexual activity—everything else you do in a dating relationship can be experienced in a friendship. And there is a lot you can do as best friends!

Let's make it fun!

1. Choose a friend of the opposite gender you enjoy being around.
2. Consider what your interests are together.
3. Rank the following best friend dates 1-10, with 1 being your favorite and 10 being fun but not your favorite. (Because the truth is, YOU bring the fun to every situation you encounter! If you come with the right attitude and the right person, any activity can be fun!)

___ Bonfire in the backyard (with Smores, of course!)

___ Compete on the Pickleball court

___ Make friendship bracelets

___ Attend a sporting event

___ Game night with the family (Monopoly, anyone?)

___ Go thrifting at multiple stores

___ Walk your dogs together

___ Have a bake-off in the kitchen

___ Learn to knit

___ Tie die matching shirts

As you engage in activities like these, you'll find yourself feeling more connected because that's what happens when we have shared experiences that aren't riddled with physical tension and distraction. Instead, you discover each other's true personalities, passions, and endearing qualities.

The Bible talks a lot about the beauty of good friendship.

PROVERBS 27:17
Iron sharpens iron, and one man sharpens another.

PROVERBS 13:20
Whoever walks with the wise becomes wise, but the companion of fools will suffer harm.

These verses stress the importance of intentionality when it comes to friendship. Think of how many people you know who just fall into friendship. The only requirement for friendship seems to be the ease of proximity—she's in my class, he's on my team, they ride my bus. Scripture urges us to be selective, choosing those who are wise and make us better people. When you are intentional about who you choose to spend time with, friendship becomes life-giving.

Here are a few questions to ask yourself as you evaluate any kind of friendship:

▶ **AM I THE BEST VERSION OF MYSELF WHEN I AM WITH HIM?**

▶ **DOES SHE GIVE EQUALLY TO THE RELATIONSHIP?**

▶ **IS HE RESPECTFUL TO ME AND OTHERS?**

▶ **DOES MY FAMILY LIKE HER?**

▶ **DO WE CHALLENGE EACH OTHER TO PURSUE JESUS?**

▶ **WHEN WE HAVE A CONFLICT, IS HE WILLING TO WORK IT OUT?**

▶ **CAN I BE MYSELF AROUND HER?**

If you are investing in a true, opposite-gender friendship—and not a "We're in denial because we are really dating but just pretending we're friends"—you'll involve other people frequently as you hang out together. You'll take in a baseball game with his family. You'll play Settlers with her brother and sister. Cosmic bowling with your band geeks? Yep. Being surrounded by others keeps you accountable to not fixate on your bestie but spread your attention and love around.

It's true that an opposite-gender friendship can move into a dating relationship. But how great would it be if the status changed after months of genuine friendship? Think of the depth your dating relationship will have because of the time and energy you put into your friendship! Whether you break up or get married, you'll both be better because of your intentional friendship!

HOW ARE YOU COUNTING ON ANY UNREALISTIC EXPECTATIONS?

Who have you been hanging out with lately? Not just in person, but in your ears?

When your parents were younger, they heard the Proclaimers say into their headphones, "I would walk 500 miles, and I would walk 500 more. Just to be the man who walked a thousand miles to fall down at your door." That sounds romantic, but realistically, that guy needs a nap and a Gatorade.

When your older siblings grabbed their iPods and plugged in their earbuds, they heard, "Hey, I just met you, and this is crazy, but here's my number, so call me, maybe." The author of that song, Carly Rae Jepsen, must've really hoped to build her contact list…or was just really bad at small talk.

Who's in your head these days? What advice and expectations about life are their lyrics giving you? The wisdom from 1 Corinthians 15:33 doesn't just apply to people we connect with in person, but also those we let in through media: **"Do not be deceived: 'Bad company ruins good morals.'"**

We're not just influenced by music but also by movies and TV shows. Think about how many times you've watched one and thought, "I totally know where this is going." There's a reason for that – you've experienced certain storylines over and over again as you've grown up. The people who make films know what we want to spend money on, so they often give us those plots…the kind where the bad guy loses, the couple ends up together, the misunderstood kid becomes understood, and AirBud scores a goal. Even the weird ones that defy that capture our interest for that very reason…they're pushing back on the expectations we've grown to have.

If you're tracking, then let's take a moment to be honest about how a song, movie, TV series, or something similar has handed you an expectation about life. For example, if you grew up watching Buzz and Woody, you might yearn for the kind of friendship they developed. If Taylor Swift's been in your head, well…first of all…sorry…she may not leave anytime soon…but how have her experiences, heartbreak, and outlook on how a dating relationship ought to be impacted how you see it?

Of course, what you think life should be like might come from your own journey or seeing what others around you have gone through. Be honest…what's one thing you expect each of these to be, and where did it come from?

- **SINGLENESS:** I expect…

And I got this from…

- **DATING:** I expect…

And I got this from…

- **FRIENDSHIP:** I expect…

And I got this from…

- **ROMANCE:** I expect…

And I got this from…

That's a powerful exercise, isn't it? Sometimes, we live our lives believing things "ought" to be a certain way, which only makes it hard when they aren't. It can even impact your relational world, too. Maybe you assume if you write and send 7,000 letters to someone you're interested in that they have to assume you're romantic…that is, until that person falls for the mail carrier who delivers them.

One of the smallest books of the Bible is the book of James. It was written by God to us through a half-brother to Jesus, born to Mary and Joseph after they were married. We know from other Bible passages like John 7:5 that he and his brothers didn't believe in Jesus. At some point, though, that changed for James, and his unrealistic expectations of who His brother was/wasn't got reset. Keep that in mind as you read this:

"Come now, you who say, 'Today or tomorrow we will go into such and such a town and spend a year there and trade and make a profit' — yet you do not know what tomorrow will bring. What is your life? For you are a mist that appears for a little time and then vanishes. Instead you ought to say, 'If the Lord wills, we will live and do this or that.'" (James 4:13-15)

Ouch. Our lives are compared to a mist here, reminding us that even a long life really isn't quite so long in the big picture of eternity. That doesn't mean what happens in these years isn't important, but is only an on-ramp. What we think matters or expect out of life may need some adjustments:

- **"I DESERVE HAPPINESS."** You won't be happy all the time, whether you're single, dating, married, or among friends… and that's okay! God instead offers us Himself on our good days and our tough days. Being tested also develops us in ways that truly grow us (see James 1:2-4, 9-12).

- **"I WANT TOTAL CONFIDENCE."** We can get so caught up in taking the first step until we know what it'll mean that we never move forward. Ask God for wisdom, then step into it (see James 1:5-8).

- **"OTHERS SHOULDN'T HAVE IT BETTER."** Comparison is a trap. When we see what someone else has, we assume that because it's more or less than us, we're worse or better than them — when in reality, God is growing that person in a different way than how He's growing you (see James 1:9-11)

- **"I CAN'T CONTROL MY TEMPTATIONS."** It's super easy to cave into your urges, and you may feel you'll be stuck doing that for the rest of your life. Be honest about what tempts you, and also be equally honest that God can be God to you in that. Do your part, too — get rid of the moldy ideas that keep putting sin in front of you and seek God instead (see James 1:13-18).

These are just a few things you can surrender to the Lord. The upside of doing that? While you don't specifically know what your future holds, you know who specifically holds your future.

What are your unrealistic expectations? Where did they come from? What will you do with them?

WHAT DO YOU THINK YOU NEED?

What is your greatest need outside of your need for food, water, and shelter? That's a big question that can have so many answers, depending on who you ask. Sleep, friendship, education, adventure, and acceptance would rank high for many. What about you?

Develop a list of your own top five needs here:
1.
2.
3.
4.
5.

When we dig deeper, we see that all humans need to feel loved, seen, known, accepted, and valued. These are needs ingrained in us from creation. God's intention, though, was that these legitimate needs would be fulfilled by Him. His love, attention, and relationship should secure us being loved, seen, known, accepted, and valued.

That's why when Jesus was asked which law was the greatest, out of all 613 Jewish laws, this is how He responded:

MATTHEW 22:37-40
"AND HE SAID TO HIM, 'YOU SHALL LOVE THE LORD YOUR GOD WITH ALL YOUR HEART AND WITH ALL YOUR SOUL AND WITH ALL YOUR MIND. THIS IS THE GREAT AND FIRST COMMANDMENT. AND A SECOND IS LIKE IT: YOU SHALL LOVE YOUR NEIGHBOR AS YOURSELF. ON THESE TWO COMMANDMENTS DEPEND ALL THE LAW AND THE PROPHETS.'"

It all starts with God. If it doesn't, life takes a tough turn. Here is another way to look at it: *We all have legitimate needs, but we try to fulfill them in illegitimate ways.* That's a loaded statement. Take a minute to break it down—what do you think this means?

Teenagers are notorious for attempting to fulfill their legitimate needs in illegitimate ways. I need to feel accepted, so I will dress or act a certain way so I can make my way into that friend group. I want to feel valued so I will enter a dating relationship I know isn't the best so I can at least feel like I matter. We all have legitimate needs, but we try to fulfill them in illegitimate ways.

When we miss going to God first to fulfill our legitimate needs, we become needy in our other relationships. We start to place expectations on friends and family that they can't meet, no matter how much they love us!

POSSIBLE SIGNS OF NEEDINESS:

- You continue to text someone even though they don't respond to your texts.
- You drop whatever you're doing when someone offers to spend time with you.
- You stalk people on social media, wondering why you weren't invited or included.
- You say things like "I miss you!" or "We never spend time together anymore!" *Imagine these being said in a whiny, needy voice.*
- You wish people would pay more attention to you in social settings.
- You find yourself making poor choices in hopes of people liking you.

WARNING: Only unhealthy people are attracted to neediness. A guy who likes to live on a power trip wants to date a girl who is needy. A girl who believes she is all that wants to be with a guy who acts like he's nothing. These relationships will certainly end badly.

TRUTH: Neediness is not attractive, it's repulsive. Healthy individuals find neediness offensive. What you think will pull or force them into a relationship actually pushes them away from the relationship!

> "ONLY UNHEALTHY PEOPLE ARE ATTRACTED TO NEEDINESS."

Read the Matthew passage above one more time. Do you see the intentionality in the order? Jesus says, love God, then love other people. When we get the order right, our relationships are healthy. When we get our foundational needs met by the One who can meet all of them, we are healthy friends, family members, teammates, and classmates.

Nobody starts the day wanting to be needy, but if we don't go to God first to fulfill our legitimate needs, that's what will happen. Then, with health and confidence, be an individual who can offer love and support in every relationship you're in! What do you need from God today to make this happen?

WHO'S (REALLY) GOING TO ANSWER YOUR PRAYER?

Can you still recite a prayer you learned when you were little? I bet you can! "Come Lord Jesus, be our guest…" "Now I lay me down to sleep…" "Rubba dub dub, thanks for the grub!" That was a great place to start, but hopefully, you've advanced in your communication with the One who gave you that grub.

Prayer is a vital part of a relationship with God. All throughout Scripture, we're encouraged to pray—without ceasing, with others, in times of pain, in times of praise, and as we cast all our cares on Him. Just like any relationship you invest in and want to grow, you talk to God and listen to Him in return.

In Jeremiah 33:3, God said, *"Call to Me and I will answer you, and will tell you great and hidden things that you have not known."* Notice how God promises to answer when we call to Him. Prayer is not just a one-way street, it's a partnership. Actually, our whole relationship with God can be seen as a partnership. You could say it's 100% God, 100% me.

God is a promise maker and a promise keeper. He will always do His 100%. He will save you. He will give you His Spirit. He will use all things for good in your life, even the hard things. He will guide, protect, correct, and sustain you. All the time. Every time. God is faithful.

God also invites us to play a vital role in His big story. He blesses us with common sense, discernment, intellect, strengths, and drive. He expects us to use those gifts to partner with Him in life. The other option is to sit around on our behinds and let the gifts He's given us go to waste. Not only is that not fun, it's an insult to the One who gave us great gifts!

Be certain, this formula does not relate to the salvation offered through Jesus' death and resurrection! That formula would look like this: 100% God, 0% me. It is only through the blood of Jesus that we are saved from our sin and brought into right relationship with God. That has nothing to do with us and everything to do with Him. As we follow Him, though, He invites us along for the ride.

A powerful example of this 100% God, 100% me theory is the account of Joshua we find in the Old Testament. As you read, look for the partnership that God offers Joshua.

"After the death of Moses the servant of the Lord, the Lord said to Joshua the son of Nun, Moses' assistant, 'Moses My servant is dead. Now there-

fore arise, go over this Jordan, you and all this people, into the land that I am giving to them, to the people of Israel. Every place that the sole of your foot will tread upon I have given to you, just as I promised to Moses. From the wilderness and this Lebanon as far as the great river, the river Euphrates, all the land of the Hittites to the Great Sea toward the going down of the sun shall be your territory. No man shall be able to stand before you all the days of your life. Just as I was with Moses, so I will be with you. I will not leave you or forsake you. Be strong and courageous, for you shall cause this people to inherit the land that I swore to their fathers to give them." **(Joshua 1:1-6)**

God was going to give it to him, but Joshua had to get his feet there. God was going to give him the land promised to his ancestors, but Joshua had to lead the people to that land. God wanted Joshua to do his 100%, and he did! And what a ride he had! (Read the rest of the story to find out!)

Each of us tends to have a default setting—bending toward letting God do all the work or believing that we can muscle through and do it ourselves. It's natural to have a default, but the goal is to bring it into balance—100% God, 100% me.

Take the space below to write out a prayer to God, asking Him to reveal to you what this formula could look like in your current season of life:

Are you willing to leave your default behind and move to balancing 100% you, 100% God?

SHIFTING BOUNDARIES: GOOD OR BAD?

If lust is weak and never satisfied, then is restraint a sign of strength and contentment?

While you're pondering that, let's talk about bowling.

What's your favorite way to awkwardly toss a ten-pound ball at a triangle of ten pins? Do you run hard and throw it with as much power as possible? Are you one of those circus performers who struts up diagonally and whips it like a curveball that almost goes off the lane…but somehow spins toward the center pin right at the end?

Or are you among the great many people who really like using gutter guards? Some would argue that these alley-long tubes or rails that keep players from failing don't belong in real bowling. The people who came up with them believed that by helping young bowlers get their balls down to the end and knock down pins, they're more likely to become regular bowlers.

This is a good way to think about boundaries in our own lives, too. Boundaries aren't meant to stop progress but to keep it going.[1]

Don't miss that when it comes to the different relationships in our lives. It's a really good thing to protect what matters. Romans 16:19 says to be excellent *"in what is good and innocent as to what is evil."*

So, let's call out the "big boundary" Christian relationships are supposed to have. We'll give you a hint – it's a physical one. Some people even wear jewelry like rings or necklaces to show they're all in on keeping it special.

If you said, "Save sex for marriage," then you win. Absolutely! This is an amazing boundary! Why would you give your whole

> Wrestling with shifting boundaries is a real thing. Galatians 5:19 says the acts of the sinful nature are "obvious" – the flesh wants what is wrong. I've had to navigate this, realizing that temptation is really about doing something that does not honor God. Once you determine this by prayer and digging into the Word of God, you need to have a potentially awkward conversation with your girlfriend/boyfriend. Be vulnerable with them and let them know you're struggling to keep things God-honoring. If that person truly wants a relationship that honors the Lord, they will listen and help shift boundaries back to an area well before the line you had previously drawn
> - Dawson, 23

---

1   Thank you to Joshua Myles for this analogy and several thoughts in this chapter.

body to those who haven't committed to giving their whole life to you through God? Sex in all its forms is a gift meant for a husband and wife. The boundaries you put up there can help you from ending up in the sexual "gutter."

What about other boundaries, though? What boundaries are worth setting up, and why, and is it okay if they ever change along the way?

Before you quickly answer what you think about that, it's important to claim why it matters:

"I appeal to you therefore, brothers, by the mercies of God, to present your bodies as a living sacrifice, holy and acceptable to God, which is your spiritual worship. Do not be conformed to this world, but be transformed by the renewal of your mind, that by testing you may discern what is the will of God, what is good and acceptable and perfect." (Romans 12:1-2)

"ONLY BY UNDERSTANDING HIS GOOD HEART TOWARD US CAN WE DECIDE TO TRUST HIM WHEN WE'D RATHER NOT."

That tells us that the starting point for amazing, helpful boundaries isn't the desire to have amazing, helpful boundaries. It begins by taking a good look at God and His mercy. Only by understanding His good heart toward us can we decide to trust Him when we'd rather not. Before we wrestle with whether or not we want to honor Him with our bodies, we get to consider 1 John 3:16, which says, *"By this we know love, that He laid down His life for us, and we ought to lay down our lives for the brothers."*

Then, after that, we get to offer our bodies to God as an act of worship. This means you choose to honor Him with what you do with your arms, hands, feet, elbow, pinkie finger…everything…including the parts of your body that are wired for physical/sexual pleasure.

Noting the order in which all of this is happening, what's next is to understand that the world is going to try to get us to cave into its broken thinking. Instead, we're to ask God to transform our minds personally and through His words. That way, whatever path we walk comes from Him. If you sum that up, then it seems like what God is saying is it's okay for your boundaries to shift…so long as those shifts move you closer to Him and preserve your innocence in a world that wants you to see and do everything:

- **SPIRITUAL BOUNDARIES MATTER:** Who is the Savior in your life, in your friendships, or in your dating relationship? It's one thing to say it's Jesus, and another thing for you to not rely on past momentum or last Sunday's sermon… but on your own or with another person actively seek Him. Hebrews 12:2 dares you to regularly keep your own eyes that much more fixed on Jesus.

- **PHYSICAL BOUNDARIES MATTER:** The more you're "okay" with doing physically before marriage shortens the list of what feels "special" after marriage. 1 Corinthians 6:18 says to "run" from sexual sin…so what does that mean when it comes to kissing? Be careful who you ask because sometimes people who just wanted to kiss and have it be okay will give you advice out of their experience and not out of Scripture. Romans 16:6 offers that it's possible to greet one another with a holy kiss, which implies a kiss can be a greeting. Proverbs 6:27-29 challenges that we can't scoop fire on our laps, though, without getting burned. Ask God what that means for you when it comes to physical boundaries that keep you healthy.

- **MENTAL BOUNDARIES MATTER:** Where are you getting advice from, and why are they giving that advice? Is it time to completely unfollow some broken people or delete things on your playlists that give you corrupted advice, like a computer virus that's infecting everything? Philippians 4:8 says to instead focus on what's pure and true… what's normal versus what's common.

- **EMOTIONAL BOUNDARIES MATTER:** We tend to turn to other people about things that we should first turn to God about. What are the things you're hoping someone else will solve for you, be it a person in your life or an "expert" from afar? Other people's voices and opinions can keep you from hearing what God wants to tell you. Bring your most precious struggles and feelings to Him first every day. Proverbs 4:23 says, **"Keep your heart with all vigilance, for from it flow the springs of life."**

- **FUTURE BOUNDARIES MATTER:** This is tricky because you are ideally only dating someone you can see in your future, but you also need to be careful in planning out your future out loud. Dating is a time of exploring how to grow with God with another person. Any talk about the future should line up with the actual level of commitment you have together while keeping an open hand to God. Jesus told a story in Luke 12:19-21 about someone making plans to build huge barns to build a grand life without realizing he hadn't accounted for what God knew about his life. Proverbs 19:21 adds, **"Many are the plans in the mind of a man, but it is the purpose of the Lord that will stand."** You don't need to be naming your future kids when you just learned each other's favorite brand of Sour Patch Kids. Talking about marriage all the time can rush you ahead of where you actually are and skip over the forming of real-time commitment. Work on the present and notice what kind of future it naturally points you to… and then determine what is and isn't healthy.

Let's say you're in a dating relationship that seems to be growing toward marriage. For the record, you're not married…until you're married. Don't play house in the meantime or let your "history" together cause you to lower your standard. One person's insecurities can end up trying to see if the other person will cross a small line in an area that's been off-limits in the relationship. For example, if the couple felt the conviction of God not to kiss until engagement or marriage, then asking the question, "Is one little kiss really a big deal?" is hurtful. Trying to seduce someone across that line in how you act or what you wear is also selfish.

Before you even think about marriage, it's key that the two of you show your love by respecting God and the convictions He's given you. While the Bible doesn't tell you in detail, "Should we hold hands tonight?" or "Is it wise to be under a blanket together watching a movie?" we do have plenty of Scripture that tells us purity is worth it. After all, the self-control you hope to have as husband and wife...to not cave into the temptations others might throw your way...begins now as a team. Never expect one of you to be the hero and carry all the burden of temptation on their own.

Psalm 37:4 encourages, **"Delight yourself in the Lord, and He will give you the desires of your heart."**

What if that doesn't mean God will act like a genie for whatever your heart desires, but that He will give you...impart into you...show you...what the desires of your heart are meant to be?

HOW CAN YOU DECIDE "NOW" WHAT WILL HAPPEN "THEN?"

"How far is too far?" This same question has probably been asked for thousands and thousands of years. Even though it's a popular question, it's not the best question when it comes to sexual relationships.

We were created by God to be sexual beings. Adults don't often lead with that, but it's the truth. That shock that runs up your arm when he holds your hand for the first time? God created you to experience that shock. The silly feeling you get in your stomach when she walks into the room? God is behind that, too.

> I've seen how easy it is to move past boundaries that haven't been firmly established or properly communicated, and it's led to hurt every time. The best relationships start with clear boundaries. These are the key steps to setting your relationship up for success.
> - Corinne, 23

But because God wants what's best for you, He has put boundaries around sexual activity outside of marriage. Boundaries aren't often high on a teenager's list of priorities. Most teenagers like eating as many Doritos as they can in one sitting. They get a thrill from staying up until 4 am playing video games. Even drinking three energy drinks in a short period of time feels exciting for a 16-year-old. Putting limits on life doesn't seem fun, but it's needed.

In 1 Thessalonians 4:3-5, the Apostle Paul lays out a solid reason for boundaries:

"For this is the will of God, your sanctification: that you abstain from sexual immorality; that each one of you know how to control his own body in holiness and honor, not in the passion of lust like the Gentiles who do not know God..."

Paul was helping the early Christians to understand that they were called to be sanctified—different, set apart. The same is true for us today; we're supposed to look different, especially when it comes to how we sexually handle our bodies. Those are some strong words that make up an intense ask from God.

How can you make this happen in your life as you date or consider dating?

STEP ONE: KNOW
Determine before you even enter a relationship how far you are willing to go physically

while still controlling your body in a holy way. Pray and ask the Lord what He would want for you in the area of sexual boundaries. Reach out to a trusted adult believer and talk through your initial thoughts with them. The best time to determine your sexual boundaries is when there is no relational or physical pressure.

STEP TWO: COMMUNICATE

As soon as possible, communicate your boundaries with the person you are dating, even interested in dating. They can't read your mind, so you need to be clear. Also, they may not be on the same page as you, and the earlier you know that, the better it is for both of you. If you both agree, you have an honest conversation to come back to as you advance in your dating relationship.

STEP THREE: AVOID

Once you have established and communicated your physical boundaries, be smart about the situations you put yourselves in. Do all you can to avoid tempting situations—like laying on a bed together, watching a movie in the basement by yourselves, or touching each other in places that shorts and a t-shirt would cover. If you're serious about your boundaries, you'll be smart about where you are.

STEP FOUR: ACCOUNTABLE

Since we were created to be sexual beings AND teenagers' hormones are running hot, it's so important to have trusted people in your corner who are helping you hold to your boundaries. As you choose someone to keep you accountable, look for someone with similar goals and the ability to get in your face if needed. Your accountability partners can't be soft!

If you take these steps, asking God for His help along the way, you can replace "How far is too far?" with "How can I please God with my body?" That's the best question! So ask it - How can I please God with my body?

EXPERIENCE: WHAT DOES PURSUING SOMEONE LOOK LIKE?

A dog who follows you around as you eat a piece of cheese. A kid selling cookies at your door who won't take no for an answer. An entire basketball team who runs hard after you when you're passed the ball. A waiter who keeps interrupting your meal to ask how you like it.

What do all these people have in common? Each is willing to pursue you.

There are more personal ways for you to do this, too. A friend gets sick, so you go out of your way to visit. A teacher or small group leader is mistreated by students, so you bake brownies with a note that says, "You're awesome!" A particular person of the opposite sex has character that lights you up and a killer smile, so you choose to sit nearby at a pool party in order to get to know each other better.

As we've already covered, neither friendship nor dating is necessary to make you whole. You can be an incredible single person who loves Jesus, lives in the woods, chronicles the lives of squirrels, and never sees anyone. You can be "whole" in this but will miss out on something God calls "better."

"Two are better than one, because they have a good reward for their toil. For if they fall, one will lift up his fellow. But woe to him who is alone when he falls and has not another to lift him up!" (Ecclesiastes 4:9-10)

WHAT DOES PURSUING SOMEONE YOU'D LIKE TO BE FRIENDS WITH LOOK LIKE?

Every friendship has a purpose to it, whether said out loud or just lived out. We "pursue" others for some reason, despite if we've never thought about it. Even when we have a starting point, like being siblings or neighbors, "something" makes us pursue each other. Try to notice this in these famous friends as you answer this question – what is the purpose of this relationship?

Famous friends	What is the purpose for this relationship?
Scooby & Shaggy	
Anna & Elsa	
Superman & Batman	
Rapunzel & Pascal	
Timon & Pumbaa	

Now, list some of your own friends and why you pursue each other as you answer the same question.

My friends	What is the purpose for this relationship?

When there's a purpose, you can push past quitting points with each other. Like, say your friend starts mocking your favorite movie or sports team – and what starts out as playful just gets ickier and more sarcastic. What if your friend is suddenly into someone you are and begins sending out vibes to that person? How about if your friend unintentionally lets you down in a way that feels personal?

Having a larger purpose for your friendship, like being Christians or wanting that person to know Jesus, can pull you through that weirdness. Just being friends because you happen to be near each other and have history, though, has less purpose to draw from.

WHAT DOES PURSUING SOMEONE YOU'D LIKE TO DATE LOOK LIKE?

Dating, like friendship, is meant to have a purpose. Think of it like transportation toward something – you get to pick what that something is and decide if you want to hop on.

The world around us says: (1) Find the right person, (2) "Fall in love," (3) Fix your current happiness and future dreams on this person, (4) If failure occurs, repeat the first three steps.

God says: (1) Know Me, (2) Walk in love, (3) Fix your eyes on Jesus and let Him guide your present and future, (4) If failure occurs, be still and know that He is God.

Obviously, the second version is better…but if you do the first one, you may have a better shot at having a date this Friday. Sure, that person might be creepy, needy, or spooky… and your entire identity can get wrapped up in them, but hey…a date this Friday!

That's the real problem – we know what's ultimately healthy over time, but we want gratification now.

So one more time, consider the type of person that would be better to date. Write out "who" this person is in terms of character and values and what the purpose of dating that individual would be.

Describe the person	What would be the purpose for this relationship?

Doing that is so incredibly important and helps you to have a better basis for friendship and dating. Be real, though – life will tend to put you on the spot with this. You may see someone and think, "WOW!" as your insides begin exploding. Assuming you're single and ready to mingle, try to remember the "Alphabet Approach" in these moments:

- **ADMIRE:** What about this person stands out to you? Freely tell God.

- **BRAKES:** What are you blind to about this person? Stop, and ask God.

- **CONNECT:** Is it wise to talk with him/her? Would your parents be okay with it? If so, say hello.

- **DISCOVER:** As you're talking with this person, what is the Holy Spirit trying to tell you? Let Him.

- **EVALUATE:** What will you now do in light of all of this? Is God saying to stop, but you want to keep going? Is it the other way around? Or are you in complete agreement with Him?

That "Connect" step doesn't have to happen in that first conversation but can be set up to happen in a group setting later. Basically, you're barely pursuing him/her before you discover and evaluate if it's worth it to keep pursuing him/her. Even if you have a few ideas, ask God to help you be creative. He invented everything and can certainly help you to question all your answers.

CREATIVE WAYS TO CONNECT AS FRIENDS, WITH A GROUP, OR AS A COUPLE

- **"DO A PICNIC"** — but what's one rule or aspect about it that could make it feel unique?

- **"GO ON A HIKE"** — but how might things get more interesting if one of you wore a blindfold?

- **"VISIT A MUSEUM"** — but could you communicate without speaking while you were in it?

- **"PLAY MINI GOLF"** — but what if you swapped out the golf ball for a bouncy ball?

- **"TRY A NEW RESTAURANT TOGETHER"** — but how could it be fun for you to write a positive ten-paragraph review of everything you liked together?

- **"COOK OR BAKE FOOD"** — but who would you give it to and why?

- **"HAVE A BOARD GAME NIGHT"** — but which two games could you combine to make a new one?

- **"SIT AROUND A BONFIRE"** — but how many different types of s'mores could you create?

- **"SHOP AT A USED CLOTHING OR THRIFT STORE"** — but what outfit could you make for each other that you were required to take fun photos of?

- **"PLAY VIDEO GAMES"** — but would you both/all be willing to play with the controllers upside down?

Those are just ten ideas, and hopefully, you see how asking one question can level things up so you see how he/she reacts to fresh experiences. Another great thing about all of these ideas is they can open up great spaces for great conversations!

WHAT TO TALK ABOUT WITH ANYONE
Hanging with friends? Going on a first date? Looking to get to know your special some-one better? Want to understand your parents or siblings better? Pursue them by asking questions that don't create a "Yes" or "No" response but help you keep chatting.

(CIRCLE) ANY OF THESE THAT YOU'D LIKE TO TRY.

- **Who** taught you how to ride a bike, and what do you remember about it?

- **What** did you like about where you grew up, and what's one thing you would have changed?

- **When** you have a day off, what's one of your favorite things to do?

- **Where** is somewhere you've traveled that makes you smile when you think about it?

- **Why** is your favorite dessert your favorite dessert?

- **How** would you describe what makes for a good book or a good movie?

- **Who** are your family members – and which Disney character is each most like?

- **What** are three things you can cook well?

- **When** do you think life gets better, and when do you think it gets worse?

- **Where** are you at on something you hope to finish one day?

- **Why** is your favorite sports team better than mine, and why are you wrong?

- **How** would you describe God to a toddler?

- **Who** are you today versus who you were 3 years ago?

- **What** is one of the smallest things you've found your relationship with Jesus impacts?

- **When** are you most a "people person," and when do you most want to be by yourself?

- **Where** do you drift off to when you have a big project and aren't ready to start it?

- **Why** do you think either of us would be a great world leader?

- **How** could someone plan a romantic date and spend no more than $5 doing it?

Now, drop one of those into a random text to someone in your contact list and see what happens!

Also, did you notice the pattern? "Who, what, when where, why, how" are great words to remember if you ever feel like you don't know what to say…especially when you're hanging out together doing something from that last section, or (if it's a dating relationship) considering being romantic based on how things are going.

FUN WAYS TO BE ROMANTIC
Don't just jump here without reading the chapter on romance. If you have, here are some extra questions to create some better answers.

- **How** could you, in less than 2 minutes, communicate you're genuinely thinking of him/her?

- **Where** might you leave little notes about what you like about him/her that he/she later finds?

- **When** would giving him/her flowers feel incredible?

- **How** could you anonymously sneak one of his/her favorite frozen treats into his/her freezer?

- **What** if you texted for two days using only emojis and gifs?

- **Where** would be a beautiful place to take a walk together?

- **Which** of his/her family members would it feel special to invest into?

- **What** if you asked what his/her ultimate meal would be and offered to make it?

- **When** might it really be inspiring and meaningful for you to pray for him/her in person about something important?

- **What's** a great joke or story about yourself you can send in an audio text message that would make him/her laugh?

- **How** does he/she need an ear to listen or a shoulder to lean on?

- **Why** would a particular compliment really have special meaning if you said it?

- **What** could you send in the mail that would feel meaningful?

- **Which** photos from the past would be an incredible photo album you could give him/her?

It's all about being thoughtful and playful through warm surprises. Try writing a few ideas of your own:

1.

2.

3.

Some people associate romance with old stories about heroes who laid down their lives for love. Today, it may look more like traveling far to surprise your crush, asking them out in front of friends, or just caring for each other in fun ways. Nothing compares to being pursued.

God models this, doesn't He? In every era of the Bible, we see Him going out of His way to let us know He wants us. Song of Solomon 8:5 gives a nod to this through inspired poetry that describes a couple who has been through a lot, yet they pursue each other through even the desert moments of life: *"Who is that coming up from the wilderness, leaning on her beloved?"*

If God has put it on your heart to pursue someone, then ask Him what it could look like so it was received well. It's tempting to want to be so romantic and incredible that it comes across as "too much." So, do you think it's about starting small or going big? How can your affection feel thoughtful and kind versus wild and explosive?

Perhaps it goes back to where we started. Is romance best after a God-honoring friendship started and formed a God-honoring dating relationship, so now all these new God-honoring romantic actions build off of it? Or is romance a "go-big-or-go-home" thing to get his/her attention?

How will you figure out which one it is?

Who or what will be your source on that?

HOW COULD YOU (AND SHOULD YOU?) ASK SOMEONE OUT?

If modern dating is an American idea (and many argue it is), then imagine if it started during early settler times (which it didn't, but play along).

First off, consider your fashion statement if you're a Pilgrim guy: black-and-white threads that say, "Hey girl…I work the fields AND milk cows!" Your massive white collar, stockings for days, and serious buckles all vibe how you're here to conquer new lands and maybe hit up a turkey dinner later.

Ladies? From the top down, you're serving looks in a snazzy bonnet over a colorless gown that shouts, "I can slay a chicken like I slay this apron, sir." Jewelry? Who needs it? You're wearing the ultimate OG "modest is hottest" flair-without-flair that tells your village you're ready to sew quilts or churn butter.

Sure, maybe you'd rather avoid this era…be it the unique expression of gender roles, lack of decent plumbing, something called "scurvy," or zero flavors of Mountain Dew. Still, there was one great thing this generation had – the town dance! Cities and settlements of people would regularly gather in local barns or open spaces to connect, chat, and dance out the ups and downs of life.

Now…imagine living in a world like that where every week offered you a natural opportunity to look into the eyes of the opposite gender without it feeling weird. Even those who weren't good at striking up conversations had a regular chance to grow their social circle… and maybe ask (or be asked) the question, "Would you like to dance?" while comfortably knowing it was, in fact, just a dance.

NO ONE WANTS TO GUESS AT IF THEY'RE BEING ASKED OUT OR NOT. IT'S KIND TO BE CLEAR."

Opportunities like this continued into other generations who also grew up having face-to-face co-ed conversations. If your interest in someone grew, all those weekly "reps" created "muscles" you could draw upon to ask someone out on an actual date, "go steady," or…churn butter together for life.

Are conversations with the opposite gender a regular part of your day? We're not talking about the number of times you've "flirted" by liking someone's post, nor the four words you've texted someone after writing four million others that you started and deleted.

ARE YOU ACTIVELY AND ENERGETICALLY BUILDING CO-ED CONNECTIONS?

In some Christian circles, there's a false belief on this topic that smells true: "If you focus on growing with God, He'll bring someone to you."

Yes, it's absolutely important to follow Jesus before jumping into anything with anyone. Otherwise, your constantly changing thoughts and emotions will lead you. Spending time with God helps you address your next steps in life, too – which also creates a clearer idea of where you're headed.

However, you can't assume that if you have regular moments with God and worship Him in all things that He's going to drop the right guy or girl on your doorstep. That's like saying, "If I open up my wallet while I read the Bible, God will fill it with cash." Um, no. The Bible itself points us in the other direction.

Proverbs 18:22 tells guys, *"He who finds a wife finds a good thing and obtains favor from the Lord."* The girl of your dreams won't magically appear and wait for you to finish gaming so she can tell you she's yours. To "find" her means you must search for her – be it by paying attention to the amazing ladies who are already in front of you, or putting yourself into as many healthy, God-honoring circles as you can (like church, serving opportunities, area ministries, Christian friend circles, etc) to "find" young women who love the Lord. It also means you "find" ways to create multiple conversations with them in an era when the local town dance doesn't regularly exist to do it for you.

Now…in light of that…how could you (and should you) ask someone out? Do you want to go for it…but are scared of being rejected? Perhaps you just don't have the "reps" from those old-time town dances. So instead, consider something awesome from your generation: video game "Easter eggs."

Imagine you're playing a Nintendo-style side-scrolling Mario game. You can certainly just go from left to right, hoping to eventually see the hero and the princess meet up. Or, you could make the most of every space you're in by jumping around in lots of different directions, all while still staying on task. If you do this, you're more likely to discover an "Easter egg" – a hidden bonus option, like an invisible block or warp pipe, that furthers the mission and gets the hero and the princess together faster.

What does that look like for you when it comes to dating? Asking someone out isn't meant to be a weird thing with a stranger you've barely spoken to, but an incredibly fun "1-UP" you discover in a great one-on-one conversation or among the Jesus-centered friendships you've formed in group settings. Is there an "Easter egg" you haven't yet noticed? Look for someone who has:

- **CHRIST:** Who is already following Jesus and inspires you to do the same?
- **CHARACTER:** Whose faith isn't just about "heaven one day," but growing each day?
- **COMMUNITY:** Who hangs out with others who cheer on faith and check for blind spots?
- **CALLING:** Who is stepping toward a future that intentionally honors God?
- **CHEMISTRY:** Who is someone who makes you light up, whom you feel attracted to?

Go in that order. It's understandable if attraction hits you, but then pause to pray. If everything else isn't there first, you'll just get interested in someone who ultimately can't hold your interest. It's incredible if that person is funny and you can do "nothing" together all day. None of that matters, though, if he/she isn't in step with you and God on the most important things about life (and eternity).

When that happens, and you find yourself sensing it may be time for an official date, then you get to let that person know with clarity what you see in him/her and how you want to spend more time together. No one wants to guess at if they're being asked out or not. It's kind to be clear.

You could say something like, "I really like you and enjoy hanging out with you. Your love for God is amazing, as is your unique affection for yellow Skittles. I trust Jesus, and I know you do, too. So I'd like to take a risk because you're worth it and ask you out on a date.

And before you answer, I want you to know this wouldn't have to all of a sudden make everything serious, but could give us some fun space to see if we might like each other in other ways. If that leads to something more than friendship, great! And if it doesn't, or if at any time you feel weird, just let me know, and we will stop "that" to keep "this" – but I have to say…I feel like "this" could lead to an amazing "that." So now, this is me asking you out on a date that I have some ideas for, but we can totally plan together and make it that much more amazing. What do you say?"

Don't panic! You don't have to memorize that. It's way too long, and you'd need to say it in your own words. You're basically asking your version of the question, "Would you like to dance?" while comfortably knowing it is, in fact, just a dance.

You can even keep it short, so long as it's clear: "I was going to check out this new smoothie place this weekend and go for a walk in the park. I think it would be fun if we both went to do this together. Would you let me take you out on a date?" Just ask in person, perhaps compliment, clarify that it is a date, and have a plan that shows you've thought about it (but are also willing to collaborate on).

Putting yourself out there like this can feel incredibly hard. There's a risk that you'll hear "Thanks, but no thanks," or "I only see you as a friend." But we promise you, regret is even harder. Might it be better to take a risk with a 50% chance of success than say nothing and have 100% chance of frustration? If you do this with honor, even if you get turned down you're one "rep" stronger.

That said, what happens if that person isn't up for the date? First off, stay calm… because if you followed the steps above, you have your own relationship with God and He determines your worth. Thank Him for filling your heart with all of who He is.
Next, know that a "no" can sting if you really do like this person. You still have two options:

- **COMPLETELY MOVE ON.** Say something like, "Alright, thanks for thinking about it. I truly value you and love how you're engaged in an epic journey with God! I'm still here for you as a friend." Then, move on while staying friends. Not lingering on it is actually a mature, attractive thing because it shows you're just fine with or without having a special someone in your life.

- **FLATTER BY PURSUING.** Say something like, "That was pretty fast, and I'll totally honor your "No" if that's how you feel. To be honest, though, I want you to feel that you're worth pursuing. I mean that. I can't give up so easily. If today you only think of me as a friend, I want to give you a few days to think of what we'd be like if I was more than a friend. Don't worry — it's not going to get weird. I'm only going to ask you once or twice more over the next week or two. I might even ask you in a fun way… because you're worth it, and I want you to feel you're worth it, as a compliment to you."

Get the idea? You don't have the town dance around you, but you do have the Kingdom of God within you. Celebrate the great godly steps and relational risks you're taking because they're wins in themselves. Whether or not you end up married to the next person you ask out, you're finding your voice there to one day potentially speak to your future husband or wife. Or maybe along the way, you'll discover a calling to stay single for a while or for life. If God leads you there, know that it'll have its own unique joys and challenges.

One more word on this — as far as "when" it's acceptable or right to do this, make sure you check with God first to evaluate your motivations: "Why do I want to date? Am I going to use this to get to know You better or to just feel affection from someone?" If your reasons are self-centered, that's an alarm. That's why your next step is to share this desire with your parents as well as some godly mentors. If they are saying you're at a point where this should be waited on, or if they're telling you that this could be okay, then follow their wisdom.

Maybe you're staring at all of this like a massive weight in the gym and saying, "I just don't have the reps to lift that." Perhaps you do, or it could be not yet. So grab what you're willing and able to lift, like investing into a lot of co-ed friendships without dating anyone so you get stronger and more at ease around the opposite sex. Also, keep working on developing yourself with God and sharing that with others. As those friendships deepen, and God shows you what's healthy for you, you won't just stand on the edge of a breakthrough...you'll already be living it, with God at the center.

So...how could you (and should you) ask someone out?

WHAT DOES ROMANCE REALLY LOOK LIKE?

How would you define "romance?"

Is it when you send the perfect emoji to a special someone? Put together a prom-posal flash mob? Make heart-shaped Rice Krispies treats? Create a lip-sync video to his/her favorite Disney tune?

Or is it bigger than that? Is romance simply when someone expresses affection to you in the way you most appreciate it? Maybe your favorite version is hearing encouraging words, having someone do special things for you, getting thoughtful gifts, having someone give you quality time, or having another person put their arm on your shoulder.[2] Perhaps it's a two-way conversation when one person can't wait to hear what another thinks. It's one thing to say, "That sunset is amazing," and another thing to add, "I like how it reminds me of going on walks with my family when I was a kid. What does it remind you of?" Boom! The second part creates an open door for that person to respond. Sharing something interesting can grow interest.

What about the flirty guy or girl? Proverbs 6:25 says it's unwise to get caught up in lust or let someone captivate you with their eyes. Proverbs 11:16 and 19:22-23 say that kindness is the best way to light up another person, especially when it isn't done to impress but when it overflows out of a satisfied life.

It could be romance is when someone pursues another with smooth certainty...where there is no second-guessing, but total all-in confidence where he/she takes the lead and pours on the charm to make it clear that there's interest. Or, quite the opposite, maybe it's when it's clear that someone is shy but pushes past it to make someone else feel special... where that first person says, "You know what? I've been thinking about the best way to make you feel special. I'm about to give you my best shot. I'm even open to your advice if I fumble, but I'm going to shoot my shot..." because just trying to say or do something sincere can throw that person off into feeling wanted, pursued and flattered.

In the Greek language that the New Testament was written in, there are several different words for love:

- **AGAPĒ:** Unconditional, selfless care and sacrifice (see John 3:16, 1 Corinthians 13)

- **PHILIA:** Brotherly/friendship affection (see John 15:13, Titus 3:15)

2 Props to relationship counselor Dr. Gary Chapman for pointing these out.

- STORGĒ: The familiar love between family members (see Romans 12:10, 2 Timothy 3:3)

- EROS: Romantic or passionate attraction (modeled in Ephesians 5:31-32)

The Hebrew language of the Old Testament offered its own version of understanding love, too:

- RAYAH: A friend or companion you hang out with (see Song of Solomon 4:7)

- AHAVA: Loving someone with your will/commitment beyond feelings (see Song of Solomon 8:7)

- DOD: Physical/romantic expressions of love (see Song of Solomon 1:2)

- RACHAMIM: Compassion for another (see Psalm 103:13)

- CHESED: Steadfast kindness (see Psalm 136:1)

While these words may be new to you, most of us think of the "Eros" or "Dod" definitions when we think of "romance." What if real romance is a combination of all the words, though? Like the ultimate combo meal of a burger, tots, carrots, grapes, chocolate milk, and sundae…with a toy, too!

Even then, it's not about creating that overnight. Within the most "romantic" book of the Bible, we read, *"I adjure you, O daughters of Jerusalem, by the gazelles or the does of the field, that you not stir up or awaken love until it pleases." (Song of Solomon 2:7)*

Might that mean that romance is less like a sprint of passion and more like a marathon of investing?

The Bible is filled with incredible examples of love being expressed from one person to another:

- **JACOB AND RACHEL:** They met, and he found her physically beautiful. Rather than just act on that, he worked for her dad for seven years to earn her hand in marriage…*"So Jacob served seven years for Rachel, and they seemed to him but a few days because of the love he had for her" (Genesis 29:20)*. That's the good stuff. It got weird when he was tricked into marrying her sister instead and had to work another seven years to finally marry Rachel. Yeah…don't do that part.

- o **In other words...this person is more than you.** Be selfless. The point of romance isn't to flatter someone into liking you but to help them feel special because God thinks they're special.

- **BOAZ AND RUTH:** These two met when Ruth was taking care of her mother-in-law after all the men in their lives had died. Boaz, a wealthy landowner, showed kindness and generosity to Ruth, which helped their relationship to blossom into love. *"So Boaz took Ruth, and she became his wife. And he went in to her, and the Lord gave her conception, and she bore a son." (Ruth 4:13)*

  - o **In other words...you are more than this person.** As you pursue him/her, you'll become sensitive to how they receive or reject it. So keep growing with God, letting your worth come from Him.

- **JOSEPH AND MARY:** This young couple became the earthly parents of Jesus, but only because they followed God beyond their feelings through some huge surprises Even after taking Mary home as his wife, Joseph didn't insist on sex, *"but knew her not until she had given birth to a son. And he called His name Jesus." (Matthew 1:25).* The trust and devotion they showed to each other wasn't just seen in the birth of Jesus, but also in raising Him and building a family life together.

  - o **In other words...God is more than the two of you.** We love because He loved first. Let all the ways you express yourself to each other stay pure. Don't let all your romance wear each other's standards down, but rather, strengthen your connection to the all-in love of God.

> I remember being in 8th grade and having a girl laugh at me for being a virgin. It was a shock to my system because I had grown up knowing that's what you were meant to do. But having peers laugh at me hurt. I thought for a moment, "Am I the weird one?" But being pure isn't weird - it's what we're designed to do!
> - Brandon, 25

Now, ready for some practical tips?

- **BE PRAYERFUL:** You're joining God in what He's doing in his/her life. Ask Him how you can be a make that person feel special today.

- **BE CONFIDENT:** You don't need to fake it. Claim who you are in Christ. Stand up straight, smile, and look him/her in the eye. How you present yourself impacts how you're received.

- **BE PLAYFUL:** It's easy as a Christian to get so serious about doing everything right that you forget this can be a real fun experience. Don't feel like every act of romance has to be so serious or so special. Go to a park together. Kick a ball. Learn to cook. Go for a walk.

- **BE CLEAR:** Communicate larger values to show you want to do life with him/her, and not just earn an "Awwww!" Holding open the door says, "I'm willing to care for you." Buying him/her dinner says, "I'd love to provide for you." Romance is meant to reflect a larger relationship that could happen or is already taking place.

If romance is caring so much about another person that you pursue them in special ways, putting their needs above your own, what are a few ways you could see yourself being "romantic?"

WHAT'S THE CHEAP, CLEARANCE RACK VERSION OF THIS?

Is the clearance rack the best place to find everything? A new pair of shoes? Yep. A dress for the Homecoming dance? Smart. An ugly Christmas sweater for the party? Perfect. A dating relationship? Not unless you're into emotional baggage and pain.

Unfortunately, teenagers often transfer their passion for a good deal to romantic relationships. If they can buy a late-night value meal at Taco Bell for cheap and feel satisfied (for an hour or so), shouldn't they be able to do the same thing with the next person they ask out?

The truth is, the best in life will cost you. The best will cost you time, effort, energy, patience, and discipline. If you want that starting spot on the team, you need to put in the effort on and off the field. You need to eat right, strengthen your body, and hydrate. If you want to restore that car, you need to rebuild the engine, strip the old paint, and find the right parts. If you want first chair, you need to practice, take lessons, and learn from those who are ahead of you. All of that takes time, effort, energy, patience and discipline.

This is especially true when it comes to relationships. God, the Creator of relationships, intended them for our good and His glory. Those kinds of relationships cost something.

It's hard to hold out for and invest in relationships when you look around and see others who seem happy with "easy." So many who are dating are in it for the appearance, fun, and physical. David knew how you feel. David was a shepherd, musician, warrior, and king. Quite a resume, right? David wrote the majority of the Psalms.

His writings are so awesome because he said it like it was. When he was mad, he let God know it. When he was happy, he shouted and danced in the streets. When he saw bad guys succeeding, he called down God's wrath on them. He was the real deal.

> "You get what you pay for" applies to every single relationship, not just things you can physically buy. In my life, I have learned that the quick, easy options end up being low quality or even harming me. Whether it be food, clothing, a friend group, or a romantic relationship, good things truly take time and dedication – there's no quick way around it. God has the best things (and people) in store for us – the more we invest in our faith, the more goodness and growth we see as we spend time with Jesus!
> - Rachel, 26

As David moved through life, he saw how things played out for those who chased after the cheap things in life. Check out what he wrote in Psalm 37:1-2:

"Fret not yourself because of evildoers; be not envious of wrongdoers! For they will soon fade like the grass and wither like the green herb."

How are those shoes you scored for $8 holding up? How does that $5 sweatshirt look after a couple of washes? Not great, right? Some would say, "You get what you pay for." When you choose the cheap and easy route in relationships, life falls apart like a cheap pair of sneakers.

David is certain there's a better way to live:

"Trust in the Lord, and do good; dwell in the land and befriend faithfulness. Delight yourself in the Lord, and He will give you the desires of your heart." (Psalm 37:3-4)

We love to jump to verse four—"He will give you the desires of your heart," but we need to pay attention to the order David gives us. First, trust in the Lord and do some good while you're trusting Him. Look around the "pasture" in which God has you right now and enjoy it. Second, take delight in the Lord and your relationship with Him, matching your heart to His. When He brings you the desires of your heart, you'll know it's the best version, not the cheap and easy version.

On the days you're tempted to say "yes" to the one asking you out because you just want to be in a relationship, are you willing to pause and remind yourself that "easy" rarely translates to the best? Are you willing to hang on tight to God and wait for His best?

WHEN IS IT TIME TO MOVE ON?

Adam and Eve had the whole relationship thing super easy, right? God made him fall asleep, he woke up, his wife was naked and unashamed in front of him, and so he started spouting off poetry.

It feels a little harder for us. We usually hit puberty around the age of 13, and many people don't get married until they're at least 30 years old. That's 17-ish years of wondering who to be friends with, if dating will be a part of your life, and how to make sure everything is healthy.

Let's say things are going decently, and you're on the verge of your friendship or dating relationship becoming a bigger deal. Should you step into the next level, or should you move on? That's a good question, but (as always) break it down into even greater questions:

- Who is this person…really…and is it someone I want to shape me long-term (and vice-versa)?

- Do our big core beliefs and small everyday values inspire each other?

- Are we good doing "nothing" together…or do we get bored and drift into "everything?"

> "SOMETIMES WE NEED TO MOVE ON—NOT BECAUSE THINGS ARE THINGS ARE GOOD AND ABOUT TO GET SERIOUS, BUT BECAUSE THEY'RE SERIOUSLY BAD."

Emotions can get thick in any relationship, too. Sometimes we need to move on--not because things are good and about to get serious, but because they're seriously bad. It's easy to let things slide if we don't want even the tiniest "good" to go away because of the larger "bad." Even when your gut's screaming, "Something isn't right!" it can feel impossible to break away.

It *isn't* impossible, by the way.

At some point in a friendship or dating relationship, it may be time to move on. You can usually spot this faster in others than in yourself, though. Thankfully, God can heal the deepest hurts that someone else may have caused you. We read, *"He heals the brokenhearted and binds up their wounds," (Psalm 147:3) and "Casting all your anxieties on Him, because He cares for you." (1 Peter 5:7)*

He also tells us to say something to those who sin against us versus just to tolerate it. Most of Matthew 18 speaks on this, from the role of forgiveness to the health of accountability. Here are some questions that might help you figure out if there's something to talk about and maybe move on from:

- **AM I LOSING MY PASSION WITH GOD SPIRITUALLY?** If they pull you away from God, it's probably time to pull away from them. Maybe you didn't see it coming because you entered into this relationship too quickly. Do you want the people closest to you to be in sync on the biggest truths of life, from who God is, what it means to be a human being, why you do whatever you do, what is and isn't a family, how you spend money, caring for others who are lost, and so on? Even if he/she doesn't personally know Jesus, it's okay to admit you may not be the best person to help him/her.

- **AM I BEING HURT PHYSICALLY?** You might want to blindly forgive or make excuses, even blaming yourself for his/her behavior. Talk with an adult you trust right away about what has happened, even if it means your friend or date will "get in trouble" for the choices they've made…that's on him/her. You saying something is up to you…so please say something.

- **AM I GETTING TAKEN ADVANTAGE OF SEXUALLY?** Is your friend exposing you to porn or half-naked social media photos of others? Do they always want to watch movies with crass content? Or are you dating and getting kissed when you don't want to? Are you being manipulated to cuddle? Even if you're in an intimate relationship with someone, no still means no. It doesn't matter if you willingly went over to see him/her – no means no. Speak up on this, too, to a trusted adult. What's happened so far may even make you feel stuck or dirty…but you're not.

- **AM I DRYING UP EMOTIONALLY?** Every person in your life will need you in some way, but some may want you to be for them what only God is meant to be. Unless you're married, you can and may need to walk away from the drama. There's enough of it out there, and you don't need to add more of it inside your heart. It can be very healthy to say, "I didn't mind listening, but there's a lot you're sorting out that I can't bear the burden of. You need to talk with someone else."

- **AM I EXPERIENCING DISHONOR SOCIALLY?** Does he put you down in front of others? Is she constantly texting or inserting herself into your life when you're doing other things? Has he told you how much you need his help to look good? How often does she grab your stuff and not return it? These are all power plays meant to make you feel like you're at his/her mercy. What if it's time to draw a line, explain that what's been happening can't continue, and move on?

We know…saying that sounds easier than it feels. When you tell someone things are changing and he/she can't have access to you like before, it'll create some tension. Let it, because within that awkwardness comes clarity and a reset. You'll get to see that much more what kind of a person this is – including if he/she respects your decision or insists on you caving into things that God wants you to move on from.

You can find the strength to do all of this by remembering that God says you're worth it. God slices through it all in 1 John 4:18, saying, *"There is no fear in love, but perfect love casts out fear. For fear has to do with punishment, and whoever fears has not been perfected in love."* The confidence He gives you can disarm any insecurity you feel in not moving on.

Now, to flip it, there are times when you may naturally move on for reasons that aren't bad. It could be that what brought you together isn't there anymore, like if you're friends because you're on a sports team. Some people will likewise have a massive crush on someone all summer while they're at camp, but when camp ends, everyone just moves on. In everyday relationships, though, sometimes you shouldn't move on. If you and someone else had a misunderstanding, it's up to both of you to come together and reconcile. Even if what he/she did was hurtful, God calls us to seek one another out. Jesus says when we do, and *"where two or three are gathered in My name, there am I among them."* (Matthew 18:20)

"FORGIVENESS IS FREE. TRUST IS EARNED. WORKING THINGS OUT IS A COMMAND."

Forgiveness is free. Trust is earned. Working things out is a command. Ideally, that means you and someone get healthier together. If he/she wants to keep things unhealthy, working things out may mean moving on…especially if he/she is always apologizing for behavior that hurts you or others.

Jesus said in Mark 12 that the most important command is to love God with all your heart, soul, mind and strength. How are any of those areas less than what they could be because of this person. Likewise, He said the second greatest command is to love your neighbor as you love yourself. That means you best love others when you also practice good self-care and love.

So how about it? Are you running out of compassion? Are you becoming watered down spiritually? Are your thoughts feeling controlled? Are you regularly giving in physically? Are you losing innocence sexually? Are you becoming someone you wouldn't choose to become?

Or, is this someone incredible…the kind of friend you want to hang out with when you do ordinary things like go to the store, hike in the woods, or get late-night tacos? Is this a dating relationship where you don't dread the next text or phone call? Could you one day see a marriage with this person that means every day in the same home together for the next 50 to 70 years?

It may be tough to move on, and that's understandable. The ache of a breakup isn't about how long you've been friends or dated but the intensity of the good or bad experiences you've shared. So what does it mean to see it all? Why would you stay with somebody because of a few positive things that don't compare to how destructive everything else in the relationship is?

When is it time to move on?

IS IT EVER HEALTHY TO CIRCLE BACK?

Can the dead be brought back to life? We know about Lazarus and Jesus, but what about the guy you broke up with last summer? Or the girl you ghosted after Prom last May? Can those relationships be brought back from the dead?

> My current girlfriend and I stopped dating for a while because she was moving, and we didn't see how a long-distance relationship would work. Later, I expressed interest in getting back together, so we had a long talk about how we could make a long-distance relationship work and worked out how we could still have regular contact throughout the year. That talk gave me the confidence I needed that our relationship could work. Relational problems won't just go away if you ignore them, but instead need to be addressed and worked through to create a healthy relationship.
> - Trent, 22

Most normal people don't enter a dating relationship planning to break up, but the vast majority of teenage relationships end up that way. There are lots of reasons for breakups…cheating, boredom, lack of time, immaturity, moving, graduating, or just a slow fade. Is it ever healthy to circle back to that relationship again?

The answer depends on what has happened in the in-between. Here are a few questions for both of you to think through as you consider circling back to the relationship for round two:

AM I A BETTER VERSION OF MYSELF THAN I WAS BACK THEN?

The issues that caused your last breakup have not magically disappeared. If you have not done some work on yourself, history will repeat itself. Don't worry, it's about progress, not perfection. Have you sought counseling to talk through issues of insecurity, abandonment, anxiety, or jealousy? Do you have a healthy view of the opposite sex? Are you paying attention to what you eat? How you sleep? How you move your body? What you allow into your eyes and your ears? All of this will prepare you for a healthier round two in this relationship!

[Theology moment: The word for this is sanctification. It's the process of God working, through the Holy Spirit, to mold and shape you to look more like Jesus. As the Spirit moves, prunes, and sharpens, you become kinder, gentler, and more joy-filled. The process starts when you say "yes" to Jesus and ends when you enter the presence of Jesus.]

ARE MY MOTIVES FOR RE-ENGAGING HEALTHY?

Some people have a hard time being alone. Some people like to take the easy way out. Some people don't know who they are unless they are with someone. None of these are good reasons for re-engaging with an ex. However, if your paths have crossed again and you can both genuinely say you are better versions of yourself, that's worth a sit down over a bubble tea. If more than a year has gone by and both of you are single, it might be worth a texting conversation. If the reasons for your breakup had to do with timing, distance, or graduation, heading out to the pickleball court for a friendly match might be just what you need!

DO MY FRIENDS AND FAMILY THINK THIS PERSON IS A GOOD MATCH FOR ME?

Many friends and family withhold their concerns about a relationship until after the breakup. (Side note: This is not a helpful tactic. If you see yellow or red flags in the relationship of someone close to you, tell them. Be kind, clear, and respectful, but tell them. It's true that love is often blind—we need to help each other see the truth.) If those in your inner circle had concerns about round one of this relationship, you must check in with them before considering stepping into the ring for round two! Listen to them—they know and love you best!

Here is an encouraging truth: If it's God's will that you be with this person, there is nothing you can do to stop it! Check out Proverbs 16:9, **"The heart of man plans his way, but the Lord establishes his steps."**

His plan is being worked out in your life. True, you could delay His will for a while (Remember the Israelites' detour on the way to the Promise Land?), but you can't stop it from happening! Are you willing to rest in that assurance while you prayerfully consider whether circling back is a good and healthy move?

WHAT IF I'M REALLY NOT INTO THE OPPOSITE SEX LIKE OTHERS ARE?

How are you different, just like everyone else?

That's a weird question, isn't it? It's true, though – you're absolutely unique…"just like everyone else." Even the smartest "experts" on adolescence (the kid/teen/young adult years) don't know you like God does.

What if you didn't have to be an "expert" as you're moving through your life right now, even as you read these words? What if what you think about yourself right now isn't "everything?"

If you're not really into the opposite sex like others are, maybe it's one of these reasons:

1. **YOU'RE NOT YET INTERESTED IN DATING.** Maybe you're not looking for another person to "complete" you (because that's God's job), or you're just having a blast growing on your own and don't want to confuse that. These are great reasons not to be totally consumed by crushing on someone. Celebrate where you're at! Keep in mind, this might be hard if you're in a circle of people who are all about talking about who's interested in who, and you feel like you're "supposed to" add to whatever they're saying. Guess what? You don't! Tweak the conversation in a new direction, and take them along with you. There's nothing wrong with you being right where you're at.

2. **YOU'RE NOT ATTRACTED TO THE PEOPLE AROUND YOU.** It might be you have yet to meet some one of the opposite sex who lights you up in all the right ways for Jesus. Again, totally fine! You can follow God and put yourself into fresh experiences that expose you to other Christians. Along the way, if you see somebody else who is in step with God and you, and you enjoy being around that person, pay attention.

In my middle & high school experience, I was constantly and easily swayed by what others thought or said about me, for better or worse… usually for worse. There was pressure to be in a relationship the way others thought it should be done and pressure to do certain things because of a boy I liked. It's embarrassing if you haven't kissed a boy yet, if you want to wait until marriage, or if you want wait to to date – you aren't fitting in. Not much has changed; I still see it today as a youth leader in conversations with students. We so desperately want to belong that it's easier to follow everyone else instead of standing firm in God's plan. I learned the hard way that what God says is right is more trustworthy than what 15–16-year-olds (and adults, too!) have to say about who I should be.
- Natalie, 25

3. **GOD'S INVITING YOU TO A LIFE OF SINGLENESS.** He'll give you a choice in this, even as He invites you into a larger calling than dating. If you're single, and you're in Christ, you are complete and can fulfill whatever your God-giving purpose is as a single person.

4. **YOU ARE MORE INTERESTED IN BUILDING RELATIONSHIPS WITH YOUR OWN GENDER.** There can be a lot of reasons for this, from your comfort level with them to some past hurt from someone of the opposite sex. Let's come back to this in a moment.

First, have you ever observed a seventh-grade football team on the sidelines of their game? Among any random grouping of boys, you'll see a 5'7" lineman weighing in at 155 pounds, standing right next to a 4'11" running back who is 99 pounds soaking wet. Same age, maybe even the same birthday month, yet moving through adolescence at a totally different pace! Where they're at today doesn't mean that's where they'll be forever, right?

Our culture pushes the idea that if you're not exactly as manly or as feminine in the same way as others around you, you're different and need to label that forever. Some even find themselves less attracted to the opposite sex than their friends are. The fact is, everyone who moves through adolescence moves through at their own pace.

Add to that the fact that you were created by God to be unique. Even more exceptional than intricate snowflakes, you were created to be "you" – different from your bestie, your sister, and the guy who sits in the back of the bus. God says in all of us is a core truth:

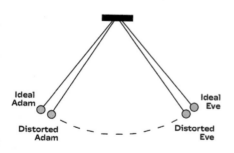

"Then God said, 'Let us make man in our image, after our likeness. And let them have dominion over the fish of the sea and over the birds of the heavens and over the livestock and over all the earth and over every creeping thing that creeps on the earth.' So God created man in His own image, in the image of God He created him; male and female He created them." (Genesis 1:26-27)

Before sin wrecked everything, including our understanding of ourselves, everything was clear. The first man and first woman reflected God in some way, with Adam being the ideal Adam and Eve being the ideal Eve. When they sinned, they each shifted away from that ideal…even just in their insecurity, to cover themselves up with leaves or to point fingers instead of owning their bad decision. Imagine this is like a pendulum[3] :

---

3 Thank you to Pastor Glen McKinney of Riverside Church for this concept.

As sin took over, this brokenness spread. Aside from Jesus, no human man has ever really been an ideal "Adam," and no female has been the ideal "Eve." Over the centuries, people have become such lovers of themselves that they have invented new ways of doing wrong: **"They have become callous and have given themselves up to sensuality, greedy to practice every kind of impurity." (Ephesians 4:19)**

That's all swung us away from our original starting point…our original God-given image. We need God's help to save us and shift us instead of letting us swing wherever we feel. Keep in mind that even the most "masculine Adam" and the most "feminine Eve" are still not at the original starting point because of sin, and we all need Jesus to save us and restore us. The same is true when there's gender confusion. Some guys may right now have interests or mannerisms that we'd assume are "Eve" things, perhaps being more emotional, sensitive, or artistic than loud, athletic, or savage. Likewise, some ladies may reflect more "Adam" qualities, as they'd rather play football and wear jeans than wear makeup and go shopping.

It feels like we're in new territory these days on what all of this means with gender issues. Categories and sub-categories pop up every day so everyone can identify themselves physiologically and sexually. You may surrounded by others who are all saying, "If you think it, that's what you are." It's the first time in history that heterosexual students who don't struggle with gender identity are being asked what their pronouns are.

It's like the newest world currency isn't crypto but identity. Not only do we want our own personal stash of it, but we also want to earn more by making everyone around us happy. Otherwise, they'll charge us with negative interest if we somehow say the wrong thing.

Ideal Adam

Ideal Eve

What if instead of just noticing this or criticizing it all, we all saw that just because an "Adam" has swung more toward the "Eve" side in interests or characteristics, he's still made by God to be an "Adam?" Like any male, he can rediscover his original and redeemed identity that's made in the image of God. Could we also invite every "Eve" to not feel like her current awareness of herself and her interests means that's who she always will be, but that she's waking up to the difference between who she feels she is versus who God made her to be? If she reconnects with God, she can become who He originally made her to be.

Of course, it's complicated. There are no easy answers. Our feelings and perspectives are multi-layered because of what we've experienced, how we're made, the sin in the world, and whatever others are doing around us. So while all of what God is telling us is true, we are in for the fight of our lives…for our lives…because it's not clean and easy, but complicated.

Oh, and for the record – we're not called to be like Adam and Eve. We're called to be like Jesus, and as the Body of Christ in all our uniqueness, we reveal Him to the world. God does point out this happens as we serve and also through the relationship of one man and one woman in marriage: "Husbands, love your wives, as Christ loved the church and gave Himself up for her…because we are members of His body. *'Therefore a man shall leave his father and mother and hold fast to his wife, and the two shall become one flesh.' This mystery is profound, and I am saying that it refers to Christ and the church." (Ephesians 5:25-32)*

Does this help? Or do you need one more way to try to understand this?

If you've ever owned a video game system, at some point, you might notice one of the game controllers has "drift" issues. That means that even if you don't touch it, it'll move the gameplay around in random directions.

Why? Because it's broken. Everyone who grabs it somehow knows, "This isn't the way it's supposed to be." Rather, "This is how it currently is."

"DRIFT" DOESN'T EQUAL INTENDED "ORIENTATION."

> "WE'RE NOT CALLED TO BE LIKE ADAM AND EVE. WE'RE CALLED TO BE LIKE JESUS, AND AS THE BODY OF CHRIST IN ALL OUR UNIQUENESS, WE REVEAL HIM TO THE WORLD."

So…instead of applauding anyone's drift, including our own, let's take whatever we have back to the Maker and let Him reset us back to His original intent.

For example, if a girl came up to you and said, "I'm ugly," would you clap for her? If a guy told you, "I'm worthless," would you agree? Of course not. We'd be affirming their drift – something that isn't true and pulls away from the work God wants to do in them.

You don't need to give big corrective talks anytime this comes up. Rather, simply share that you understand they currently feel like they're drifting into a conclusion about themselves that feels true, but may not be, and you have your own version of that…and all of us are invited to bring that to Jesus, who really is God, and really is our Savior, and really can transform us.

As it relates to why you may or may not be interested in the opposite sex, keep in mind that among all the reasons mentioned earlier, God does, through the Bible, affirm singleness, and He also affirms waiting to be in a relationship with someone who is worth waiting for...but He doesn't affirm caving into anything outside His design of "one man and one woman." He does give us free will to live outside this design, but He still speaks up against it. Even all the Old Testament kings who had multiple wives were warned not to cave into culture or lust.[4]

Confusion is confusion. Temptation is temptation. Sin is sin. They may all scream loud things about who we are and "must" do, but there are truer things about us than wherever our pendulum has swung. Drift is a part of all of our stories, and it's a part that needs to be humbly laid at the feet of Jesus.

Be specific...write this out:

How are you drifting...and what if you let God reorient you?

IS ANY OF THIS NORMAL?

Throughout this book, you've seen some incredible opportunities of how you can live differently if you're single, journeying through dating, forging friendships, or attempting romance. God is so good, and He's shown you some incredible things! Still, you might wonder, "Is any of this normal?"

Hang on…how are you using that word? What if you've been using it the wrong way your whole life?

"Normal." Try to define it. Some might say, "It describes the way things are." Is that correct? As you look around at the world…would you say things are "normal?" What would Jesus say if you asked Him the same question?

You actually already know the answer. Think about it – when something goes wrong or you see someone mistreated, you swell up and yell out, "No! This isn't the way things are supposed to be! This is not normal!"

A deeper, truer way to understand "normal" is as a noun – what God originally created life to be for every person, place or thing – versus an adjective that describes how life just ended up commonly being.

He created us to be more than who we assume we are. The sin in this world and in us blurs that and warps how we define ourselves. We end up describing "normal" through our experiences…by what is "common."

But what is "common" is not what is "normal." "Normal" is the original reference point of Genesis 1-2. "Common" is what happened after that. We tend to mix the two up despite knowing the truth deep down inside.

"For His invisible attributes, namely, His eternal power and divine nature, have been clearly perceived, ever since the creation of the world, in the things that have been made. So they are without excuse. For although they knew God, they did not honor Him as God or give thanks to Him, but they became futile in their thinking, and their foolish hearts were darkened. Claiming to be wise, they became fools, and exchanged the glory of the immortal God for images resembling mortal man and birds and animals and creeping things." (Romans 1:20-23)

Now that we've reclaimed that word (seriously, imagine if you started using it that way, and only that way) is any of what you've read about God's plan for your life in any of these areas "normal?"

Absolutely. Anything God says is normal, even if no one agrees with it.

By the way…why are you asking? "I didn't," you might say. "It's the title of your chapter, Slick." Spoiler alert – each of these chapters comes from conversations we've had or overheard with people of all ages who are asking these questions. If you haven't worded it this way before, you may have instead asked a deeper cut of the question, "Being single like this…dating like this…friendship like this…romance like this…is this worth it? Is it normal" Ah, now you're getting into the real issue.

A common question we ask growing up is "Am I normal?" It's not in itself a bad question, but it can come from our fears or insecurities. Nobody really wants to feel like they're different in a bad way, as if there's something wrong with them. So much of life already makes us feel like an outsider.

Then again, what if you could pick the kind of outsider you get to be? Like, what if your life could show others what's possible in a way we all don't understand is possible. By trusting God, giving your life to Jesus and living through the Holy Spirit, something actually changes inside of you that others see! Galatians 5:22-23 says the "fruit" of that is like the ultimate superfood…for as you invite God to fill every part of you and your life He personally grows in you a deeper love, joy, peace, patience, kindness, goodness, faithfulness, gentleness and self-control. These take time and an ongoing invitation for God to keep all of this blooming inside of you, yet as you do, He can powerfully change your journey through singleness, dating, friendship, and romance:

- Indifference and rejection may be common…Love is normal, and God offers it.

- Comparison and jealousy may be common…Joy is normal, and God offers it.

- Grumbling and stress may be common…Peace is normal, and God offers it.

- Demanding and frustration may be common…Patience is normal, and God offers it.

- Sarcasm and selfishness may be common…Kindness is normal, and God offers it.

- Sin and pretending may be common…Goodness is normal, and God offers it.

- Cheating and pornography may be common...Faithfulness is normal, and God offers it.

- Anger and abuse may be common…Gentleness is normal, and God offers it.

- Lust and recklessness may be common…Self-control is normal, and God offers it.

What do you like about what God says is normal?

Please, please don't miss this, though…none of this is about you trying to just "be normal." That's like a dead tree hoping someone nails apples onto it. It might look fruitful, but it's dead.

The real journey is trusting in Jesus who was nailed on a tree for your sin to bring you to life in Him. It's possible to appear to be doing the right thing yet not be right with Him… to nod your head to a standard someone handed you versus receiving that conviction from God. This is why some couples cross lines they said they'd never cross – one or both of them said they were on board with a particular value, but it was just them trying to do what's right until they ran out of their own strength.

This is why it's so important to invite God into every part of who you are and notice Him in every moment. He gave us His Holy Spirit to live inside of us, and He wants to make you fruitful from the inside out. With relationships and sex, for example, it's not just about avoiding crossing lines physically or keeping up appearances, but letting Him rescue us from how we think or approach temptation:

"You have heard that it was said, 'You shall not commit adultery.' But I say to you that everyone who looks at a woman with lustful intent has already committed adultery with her in his heart." (Matthew 5:27-28)

To illustrate this, Jesus used the object lesson of a body to say that if there is something attached to us that's causing us to sin, it's better to cut it out of our lives then tolerate it. That means it's normal to not date someone who's bad for you when everyone else seems to be in a relationship…it's normal to step away from something that feels good in the moment but is creating future heartache over time…it's normal to not scroll away into bad places on your phone but get accountability for it.

When the curtain of this world lifts, we'll see that God's Kingdom has been here the whole time, buried underneath our temptations and struggles. Dating or marrying someone won't fix you anymore than being a moral single person will. We are all, without Jesus, merely sinners awkwardly attempting to survive, realizing the impossibility of that task. Life can't just be about the flood of feelings we get from fancy date nights or flirty texts. Life comes from Christ, and the closer we walk with Him the sweeter our singleness, dating, friendships, and romance can become.

How might embracing God a little more help you reclaim what's normal?

EXPERIENCE: CAN I SAY THAT?

What was the first word you ever said? Have you heard the story from your parents? Is it marked down in your baby book? Maybe it was "No!" Or "Mine!" Or "Poopy!" What's for certain is that you've added to your vocabulary significantly since then! Some of you get in trouble in class every day because of how much you put that vocabulary on display!

Have you lived long enough to notice that there are words people love to use and words people cringe at? For instance, you might love to say the word "ramifications," but cringe when someone throws out the word "moist." (Sorry!) Just for fun, in the proper sections below, write out the words or phrases that make you happy and the ones you would like to eliminate from the English language:

Happy words	Cringey words

Words are a beautiful gift from God! Have you ever paused to think about and be thankful for the way we communicate? How we are able to express our joys, frustrations, and feelings? Animals don't have this luxury, just humans. But wouldn't it be so fun if your dog or cat could chat it up with you? If you could know exactly what they were thinking and feeling? Maybe in heaven…

As amazing as the gift of communication is, it can also be complicated, especially in relationships. Even though words should be used to clarify and encourage, many times they confuse and hurt. We've all been confused and hurt by words in our lives. Is this just a reality in this sinful, broken world, or is there something we can do about it? In the New Testament book of James, the author reminds us just how powerful our tongues can be:

"If we put bits into the mouths of horses so that they obey us, we guide their whole bodies as well. Look at the ships also: though they are so large and are driven by strong winds, they are guided by a very small rudder wherever the will of the pilot directs. So also the tongue is a small member, yet it boasts of great things. How great a forest is set ablaze by such a small fire! And the tongue is a fire, a world of unrighteousness. The tongue

is set among our members, staining the whole body, setting on fire the entire course of life, and set on fire by hell." (James 3:3-6)

It's as if James was writing to us now, isn't it? Comparatively, your tongue is so small compared to your bicep, and yet it causes a lot of issues. In the box below, describe three situations you have been in and how your tongue behaved. For instance: My teacher called me out in front of the class for not having done the assigned reading...I responded with sarcasm, "Well, if I didn't have a life like you..." (Not that you would ever say something that cutting—just trying to help you get going!)

How are you doing with the taming of your tongue? Do you have control of it or does it have control of you? Often, in opposite-gender relationships, we seem to lose control of what we say and how we say it. For a lot of reasons, we don't practice emotional integrity. This term, emotional integrity, means communicating our emotions in a way that is honoring to God, others, and ourselves. This can be a challenge when your emotions are so intense and all over the place as a young adult!

If you are willing to pursue emotional integrity as a single or dating person, here are five truths to guide you in that pursuit:

1. THE 24-HOUR RULE CAN SAVE LIVES, EMOTIONALLY SPEAKING.
With the speed of technology, we are so quick to respond to texts, posts and comments. Emotional integrity often calls for a delayed response. Whether it's an invite to dinner and a movie, an ask for a favor, or a YOU ARE HOT message, take a breath and take 24 hours before you respond. You will be much happier with your response than in the moment.

2. LOVE IS NOT A FEELING, IT'S A COMMITMENT.

We use the word "love" so loosely in our culture. How can one love their sweet 78-year-old grandma AND love flaming hot Cheetos? Is that the same kind of love? Our use of the word love should carry significant weight as it describes a commitment to the betterment of another person. You can really like the sting of those Cheetos, but love should be reserved for a person you are committed to for the long-haul.

3. JUST BECAUSE IT'S TRUE DOESN'T MEAN IT SHOULD BE SAID.

So often, when something comes to our minds, we just say it. We don't think about what we're saying, how we're saying it, or the damage it might cause. Some things are best unsaid. Is it true your friend gained unwanted weight over the summer? Yes, it's true. Does it need to be said? It does not. Every feeling and thought you have should be run through this filter: Is it kind, necessary, and helpful? If not, keep it to yourself!

4. YOU CAN AND SHOULD SAY "NO."

When you are first getting to know someone—a friend or a potential date, it's natural for you to want them to like you. This often tempts you to say "Yes" to things you would normally say "No" to. Any relationship that is based in pressure is not going to be a healthy relationship. So, learn to say "No" confidently to anything that contradicts your beliefs, makes you feel uncomfortable or unsafe, or doesn't honor God, yourself, or the other person. Anyone worth being with will respect your "No."

5. WHEN APPROACHED RESPECTFULLY, NO TOPIC IS OFF LIMITS.

Relationships often fail for lack of clear communication. When we respectfully communicate our needs, boundaries, desires, hopes, and feelings, the relationship is better for it. Likewise, when you give space for someone else to do the same, you are investing in a healthy relationship. Topics like pornography, sexual boundaries, past mistakes, and family dynamics not only should be talked about, they must be talked about!

REVIEW THE FIVE TRUTHS ABOVE AND TAKE SOME TIME TO ANSWER THESE QUESTIONS:

Which of these is the easiest for you to follow and why?

Which of these would be a challenge for you to practice and why?

With God's help, you can tame your tongue and experience healthier relationships! You can live into the truth in Proverbs 16:24: *"Gracious words are like a honeycomb, sweetness to the soul and health to the body."*

SINGLE, COUPLE, GROUP, UGH...

WHAT'S HAPPENING AROUND YOU RIGHT NOW IN THE SPACE YOU'RE IN?

Use all of your senses. Quiet your breathing and listen to pay real close attention to the sounds around you. What do you hear now that you didn't hear a moment ago?

Next, stand up, turn around, and try to see something in your room that wasn't in your line of sight until you saw it. Why is that thing there? What's special about it?

It's time to take a big whiff of the smells nearby. Maybe lean into something and inhale, or pull your shirt to your nose and smell it. How would you describe the scent of that thing?

Ready to touch something? Find something that you can put your whole hand on. Feel it as you palm it, and notice any textures that rub up against your fingers. Describe that here.

Finally, you're going to lick something. If there's something tasty near you, go for it. Otherwise (and this may be gross) lick the back of your hand. What did that taste like?

One of two things just happened you either totally lit up your insides and became that much more aware of the space around you...or, you blew off the assignment, saying, "I don't need to do that. I know what that's all like." (How clever. You're an expert. We'll talk more about that in a moment.)

WHAT'S HAPPENING AROUND YOU RIGHT NOW IN THE RELATIONSHIPS YOU'RE IN?

There's that one single person you know. What is that individual doing to blow off steam these days? How about that couple who started using the word "love" on the first date? Why was that the case? Don't forget the friend group you socialize with and all its spoken and unspoken expectations. How did it end up becoming what it became, for better or for worse?

GO DEEPER. What is that single person going to do this Friday, and why? How might that couple need a really good friend right now? What if your friend group became amazing with just one tweak?

GO EVEN DEEPER. What true or false beliefs does that single person have about self-worth that no one else knows? Does that couple have a healthy next step they want to take, are they just floating out there, or are they on the edge of a bad choice? Why does your friend group talk about honoring God but make a lot of off-color jokes that no one ever calls anyone out on?

GO EVEN, EVEN DEEPER. Come up with your own question to ask...

- About the single person:

- About the couple:

- About the group:

"GOD'S WAY IS GOOD AND PERFECT."

Now, one of two things just happened – you either totally lit up your insides and became that much more aware of the people around you...or, you tried to blow off the assignment and then couldn't, because no one is the expert on anyone they claim to be.

Of course, you'd never with your words say you're an expert out loud...but you likely believe it. You think about how all the single people, couples, and groups of people in your life ought to be (and who you *ought* to be, respectively) and end up saying, "UGH!"

Maybe because you have a lot of advice to give them if they'd listen?

Maybe because you see their blind spots and want to point them out?

Maybe because you are sort of bothered by where you're at?

We all need some schooling on relationships. You've probably learned a lot about some of this, but you don't know everything. Neither do the people around you. It's possible that even the older siblings or single adults in your life are acting more immature than you and your friends.

God's way is good and perfect. Not everyone fully understands this, though. Most people are just trying to survive the moment and sort out any of their overwhelming thoughts and feelings without getting stuck. We end up believing certain lies along the way. What would you say to someone who believed any of these myths?

- Myth: Being single is like being in "time out" while everyone else plays.

- Myth: The only way to be significant is to have a significant other.

- Myth: Better to avoid the friend group drama than try to change it.

GO EVEN, EVEN, EVEN DEEPER. You have a personal Savior. You also have a personal enemy. Jesus said in John 10:10, *"The thief comes only to steal and kill and destroy. I came that they may have life and have it abundantly."* If the enemy, Satan, can't get you to hate God, what if he's fine getting you to hate the life you're in or be exhausted with the people around you?

WHAT'S HAPPENING AROUND YOU RIGHT NOW IN THE WAR YOU'RE IN?

Yikes! We know that sounds really, really intense. We wouldn't point it out if it wasn't true. And what's even crazier is God says it's possible for you to experience tremendous joy in the middle of all of this.

One of the longest passages in the Bible on the joys of marriage, family, people in our work circle, and how everyone pitches in on it, is found in Ephesians 5:21-6:9. You should totally read it – it has everything in there for husbands, wives and kids. Lots of people turn to it for wisdom on all these relationships, and you can learn a ton that you could even apply into singleness, dating, and more.

Right after that, though…literally, the very next thing…we're told this:

"Finally, be strong in the Lord and in the strength of His might. Put on the whole armor of God, that you may be able to stand against the schemes of the devil. For we do not wrestle against flesh and blood, but against the rulers, against the authorities, against the cosmic powers over this present darkness, against the spiritual forces of evil in the heavenly places." *(Ephesians 6:10-12)*

Is the placement of that next to all the relationship stuff there for a reason? As it relates to your relationship status, will you just sit around on the receiving end and be naturally frustrated? Or are you willing to get proactive spiritually and study what putting on the full armor of God means?

What if you took the time to see the spiritual side of the relationship drama around you? If you took a moment to "sense" how they're in the same behind-the-scenes battle you are, would it change how you spent time with others or what you said about them? How different would your prayers be if you knew you were asking all of God and heaven to speak life and truth into the people around you?

How could you help them see what God wants them to see?

Ask God, and write down in as much detail as possible your best sense of His response here…

WHAT'S HAPPENING AROUND YOU RIGHT NOW?

EXPERIENCE: WHAT IN THIS BOOK IS WORTH IGNORING (BUT NOT DISMISSING)?

Aw…it's the last part of this book.[5] Does it maybe feel like the last day of camp, and we're all about to get picked up and head out from this amazing space we've been in together? We're all hugging, singing off-key songs, taking selfies, making promises to write/text/video chat, and doing our super secret handshake because it feels like we're not going to see each other for a long, long, long time.

That is, until we all end up at the first Chick-fil-A outside of camp and go, "I didn't know you were coming here, too!!!! Want to share some nuggets?"

That's kind of what we thought this last experience could be like. Our official time together may look like it's over, but maybe the journey we're all on isn't.

Let's share some nuggets.

However, before we do, we invite you to consider what's worth keeping and what's worth tossing. Sometimes, when we're at a restaurant and we're looking at those nuggets, we also see some crumbs that are really nothing more than balled-up grease. "Those are the best part!" someone out there named Randy just said. Not according to your doctor…or your toilet. 'Nuff said, Randy.

In fact, you know what would be even stranger than listening to Randy? Bringing your own crumbs to that feast. It sounds weird, but can you imagine, before eating your Chick-fil-A, you took out a container filled with old greasy crumbs from past meals and poured it all over that Christian chicken?

Be quiet, Randy! You're being gross. Go lick some sardines while you're at it.

Sifting out the crumbs from nuggets is like sifting out the human stuff from the God stuff in this book. If you went through this with others, for example, someone may have argued a strong thought that sounded meaty but was really just crummy. Perhaps they stated a positive value about purity that began with "You should…" or tried to devalue God's truth somehow by starting with "I don't think it's a big deal if…" – both are human-sized values that may mean well, but end up confusing everyone.

---

5   Except for the amazing opportunity after these few pages – don't miss that!

We'll own our part in this, too. We wrote an imperfect book to point you to the perfect God who perfectly loves the imperfect you that you are. Some things you've read might've felt more familiar or relatable because of your own background or stage of life. Other things may have seemed kind of strange. We're sorry if we accidentally handed you any crumbs. We may have also offered you a nugget that wasn't fully-cooked yet. See if you can find something in God's Word that will properly heat it up for you. You can even put some Chick-Fil-A sauce on it. We won't be offended.

Let's pause right here for a moment...

WHAT ARE 3 TO 5 ABSOLUTE NUGGETS YOU FEEL GOD HAS GIVEN YOU THROUGHOUT THIS BOOK?

1.

2.

3.

4.

5.

What crumbs from this time, from someone else, or from your past should now be set aside?

What we're after here is something we shouldn't probably do as authors. We're trying to get you to think about God more than you think about us...to get into His book more because of this book, even if it means putting this book to the side. Sure, we'd welcome your glowing reviews online and enthusiastic recommendations to friends if you think this would be valuable to them. They'll eventually get to this very same part of the book, too, and hear our deepest hearts on all of this.

NAMELY, IT'D BE EASIER FOR YOU TO JUST WALK AWAY FROM THIS BOOK WITH A BUNCH OF NEW STANDARDS YOU'LL TRY TO LIVE OUT THROUGH YOUR WILLPOWER VERSUS ASK GOD NEW QUESTIONS ABOUT ALL THESE NEW ANSWERS...AND WE'D RATHER SEE YOU GET MORE INTERESTED IN AND MORE DEPENDENT ON GOD HIMSELF.

What if the greatest thing you could do right now is look at all those nuggets you wrote down (and consider the ones bouncing around in your head)…

and ignore them for a moment (but not dismiss them)…

so you make sure Jesus leads you forward and the standards on their own don't?

Does that make sense? Are we losing you?

☐ No, I'm totally following this   ☐ Yes, I'm a little lost   ☐ Maybe, and I want Chick-fil-A

Alright, let's go back to Chick-fil-A. There you are, sitting there with your nuggets. You even tell your friend, "I have some nuggets." Your friend says, "Me, too. Aren't nuggets amazing?" You say, "They sure are. Especially these. They're made from the most natural chickens who weren't ever in cages but who roamed the wilderness like ancient savage chickens, breathing in air that was imported from a tropical rainforest and walking on dirt that came from a tribal village untouched by the modern world. An Italian monk who's never raised his voice in his life looked after them, whispering words of affirmation to them each day and reminding them how special they were. To not make any chicken feel superior or inferior to the others, he called them all Randy."

"Mhm," your friend says.

So there you are, just talking and staring at your nuggets.

Just. talking. and. staring. at. your. nuggets.

What good is that doing for you? Nothing, right? Until you consume them and let them become a part of all of who you are, they're just pretty poultry. So the best thing to do is eat them, right?

Maybe. But then what? You're out of nuggets, aren't you?

What if, just as you were about to eat, a man walked over and says, "Hi! I oversee all the Chick-fil-A restaurants in this state, and I'm feeling generous. Would you like free Chick-fil-A for life? It starts the moment we become friends. What do you think?" You pause. You look at his nametag. It doesn't say Randy. He looks legit. It's such an overwhelming offer.

You have two big options: (1) You can keep eating your nuggets and ignore him, or (2) You can, for the moment, ignore your nuggets (but not dismiss them) and build a relationship with him.

Which option would you choose?

☐ I want to eat now   ☐ Free Chick-Fil-A for life, of course   ☐ My name is Randy

The reason this matters is because God is with you everywhere. We may hear or say things even in church gatherings that confuse this reality, like "I was feeling confused and lost, and then God showed up!" Can we stop saying that? Because God was already there. He's always with you. You may have just noticed Him or experienced Him in a fresh way…when you showed up to Him.

WHY MIGHT IT HELP YOU OR OTHERS IF YOU DROP THE "GOD SHOWED UP" LANGUAGE?

The reason it matters that God is with you everywhere is that you will, at some point, get tired of doing the right thing. Even if you don't fully walk away from that, some days may just seem harder. This is why Galatians 6:9 says, *"And let us not grow weary of doing good, for in due season we will reap, if we do not give up."* Why does it say to not become weary in doing good? Because it's possible to become weary in doing good! Your choice with this is the same as the choice you'd face in the restaurant – eat the nuggets or build a relationship with the One who will keep giving you nuggets. With Him, you can practice discernment – the art of sifting through the old crumbs and the new crumbs to uncover the real food He wants to feed your life with. He'll help you turn information into wisdom as you recognize what lines up with Truth while intentionally setting aside the lies. Even things that are true all the time may take you another season or two of life to recognize that.

You're going to get some pushback, too. Some people will hear what you're being offered and say, "You already have what you need. Eat the nuggets." Others will say, "Say 'YES!' to this guy already!" One guy might yell, "This is stupid. Let's go to McDonald's."

And you'll say, "Be quiet, _____!"[6]

"Indeed, all who desire to live a godly life in Christ Jesus will be persecuted, while evil people and impostors will go on from bad to worse, deceiving and being deceived. But as for you, continue in what you have learned and have firmly believed, knowing from whom you learned it and how from childhood you have been acquainted with the sacred writings, which are able to make you wise for salvation through faith in Christ Jesus. All Scripture is

6 (fill in the blank – you know the "Randy" that goes here)

breathed training in righteousness, that the man of God may be complete, equipped for every good work." (2 Timothy 3:12-17)

What are a few nuggets from this that stand out to you, maybe because God is trying to get your attention on them?

1)

2)

3)

So how could you stay teachable and open to God?

Think about the last time someone tried to set your straight on something. What did you become in that moment? Teachable or frustrated? Did you defend with a spirit that said, "Yeah, I already knew that, okay?" Or did you slow down, open up, and grab a paper and pen?

Seeking God is kind of like that. You either sense Him trying to tell you something and shut Him down because you already "know better" (which is possible if you like your current version of Christianity and don't want to level up but want to show that you do "good things")…or you slow down, open up, and grab a paper and pen.

As end this book, we'd like to provide you the space. After reading this, are you a little more of an "expert" on being single, dating, friendship, and romance…or are you now more open to grabbing hold of God and growing your relationship with Him?

Maybe you realized what you "should do" or "shouldn't do." Great. Ignore that for a moment (but don't dismiss it). You may have in these pages discovered a "YES!" "NO!" or "WAIT!" – again, good…ignore that for a moment (but don't dismiss it). Perhaps you have a favorite part that you can wait to reread by yourself or with others. Super. Ignore that for a moment (but don't dismiss it).

Also, we may have missed something. It's natural for a book to leave you with unanswered questions or unresolved tensions. That's great, because we're not leaving you to wrestle with it alone but with God. If anything stands out to you that we missed, ignore that for a moment (but don't dismiss it).

We'd like to now spark some curiosity, conversation, and further questions between you and God. We'll give you a few prompts to serve as a springboard to spend the next moments with Him writing out a conversation and listening for anything you sense Him telling you.

First, recognize God. Pick a Name of His that you most appreciate now…"Lord," "Creator," "Savior," "Father," "Spirit," "Rock," "Counselor," – and then write out all that you appreciate about Him. Remembering Who you're talking to will shape what you say after that.

Dear _____,

Next, pause and ask Him to tell you the great, deeper identity He sees in you. As you slow down and listen (don't rush) be like a catcher's mitt. Receive whatever He pitches you. Then, write it down here.

I sense You want me to hear that I...

Now, share your takeaways from this journey and ask Him to give you some questions that will help you explore those takeaways even more.

A takeaway:	A question for that takeaway:
Example: Encourage my friends each day.	Example: What happens if I do? What happens if I don't?

Finally, invite God to keep speaking to you and leading you, and be specific about how you will seek Him over the next seven days (and maybe beyond).

Up to you on this one — maybe it's a P.S. to your prayer. If you get married some day, write out a specific prayer to God for your future spouse and date it. Maybe one day you'll show it to him/her. Or maybe you'll stay single and the prayer you write for him/her is a prayer for you to live out. Either way, here's the space for it:

What you're creating in all of this is a lifelong learning commitment — not to us, or even to yourself, but with the Lord…*"For from Him and through Him and to Him are all things. To Him be glory forever. Amen." (Romans 11:36)* In doing so, you remember that the value of your time in this book is not just in its content but also in the conversations and ideas it'll inspire you with in the years to come.

Thank you for letting us join you on this journey. It might be helpful to remember that we can all totally meet up with each other and Jesus by just flipping back and revisiting everything we've worked through. Maybe it'll happen as you walk through something complex in life, and you come back here to sort out whatever is unclear with greater Truth. What you've discovered over these past several weeks might just help your future self embrace God again and set aside the crumbs again.

It'll be like surprising each other at Chick-fil-A just outside of camp. We'd love to meet some of your friends, too. Maybe even now you want to hit us up and let us know what you want to talk about. If we hear from enough of you, maybe we'll even write a second book. Our working title could be "Single, Dating, Friendships, and Romance 2: Electric Boogaloo." (If that doesn't make sense, don't worry. We know it's hilarious. If someone said it wasn't, you know what to say.) Be quiet, _____!

With gratitude,

Heather Flies & *Tony Myles*

Instagram: @heatherflies @tonymyles

HOW TO KNOW JESUS

Please don't miss this. It'll change everything if you mean it!

The most important decision you will ever make in your entire life is to say "YES!" to Jesus Christ and begin a genuine relationship with Him.

No, we're not talking about if you like God, nod your head in church gatherings, or go through a class to give a thumbs up to the traditions of your faith. Those are great starting points, and you can build on them. Jesus didn't say those would save you, though. Pay attention to what He did say, and what was said about Him:

"I am the door. If anyone enters by Me, he will be saved." (John 10:9a)

"I am the way, and the truth, and the life. No one comes to the Father except through Me." (John 14:6)

"If anyone would come after Me, let him deny himself and take up his cross and follow Me. For whoever would save his life will lose it, but whoever loses his life for My sake will find it." (Matthew 16:24-25)

"But to all who did receive Him, who believed in His name, He gave the right to become children of God..." (John 1:12)

"Because, if you confess with your mouth that Jesus is Lord and believe in your heart that God raised Him from the dead, you will be saved." (Romans 10:9)

No matter where you find yourself with that, this page is for you. Maybe you've turned to this page, having never entered into a saving relationship with Jesus. Maybe you already have a saving relationship with Jesus and need to be more committed to making Him known and sharing His story with others.

UNDERSTAND WHO GOD IS.
God is the Creator over everything (Genesis 1:1), and He personally created everything - even you (Psalm 139, John 1:1-3). He is good and perfect in all His ways (Psalm 18:30), being completely "holy, holy, holy" (Isaiah 6:3) and love (1 John 4:16). If you put all of that together, God is over us and beyond us, yet approaching us and with us. He rules over everything with purity, and He loves us with character that is 100% right.

OWN THAT YOUR SIN IS REAL AND CAN'T BE SOLVED ON YOUR OWN.
Imagine growing up in a home or apartment that has imperfections, creaks and broken-

ness that over time become more obvious. Our lives are the same way – we're all sinners (Romans 3:23), born into this world separated from God because of the decisions of the first humans (Genesis 3). Since God is perfect, when we think, say, or do something that goes against His ways, that "sin" only adds to the gap between us and this world. All sin is rebellion against the Lord (Ps. 51:3-4), and the only right penalty for our rebellion is for that separation to last forever. This is a "death" that's both spiritual and physical (Romans 6:23), and we're completely unable to save ourselves.

GRASP THE TRUTH THAT JESUS IS THE ONLY ANSWER TO YOUR SIN PROBLEM.

Jesus is an equal Person of the Trinity – God the Father, God the Son, and God the Holy Spirit. He came to earth to live a perfect life, love us in person, and show us what's possible, to then willingly die on the cross to satisfy the penalty of our sin, serving as the once-and-for-all perfect sacrifice in our place (Matthew 1:18-21). This was a gift that we couldn't earn but could receive, for only Jesus could do this (John 3:16-17, Romans 6:23).

BELIEVE IN YOUR HEART THAT JESUS IS WHO HE SAYS HE IS, AND INVITE HIM IN.

We are not "good people" because of what we try to do, because all our attempts at this are still dirty (Isaiah 64:6). The only way that we can be saved from our sin problem is to believe that Jesus is who He says He is, and that His death and resurrection accomplished what He said it would accomplish. When we put our faith in Jesus as our Savior, we're saved from the penalty of our sin – that eternal death. This is only possible by God's grace through faith in Jesus. We can't do anything to earn our salvation (Ephesians 2:8-9).

COMMIT TO LIVE LIFE FOLLOWING HIM THROUGH THE HOLY SPIRIT.

This is so amazing! When you come to trust your life to Jesus Christ, your life is completely renewed and freed from the effects of sin. You are a new creation! (2 Corinthians 5:17, 2 Peter 1:4)! You don't have to try to do life in your own power, but get to do it through the Holy Spirit who comes to live inside of you…because God wants to personally love you and lead you and empower you from the inside out (John 14:7, Romans 8:15-1, Titus 3:5)!

TAKE YOUR NEXT STEP – TO SAY "YES!" TO JESUS, AND THEN TO SHARE THIS WITH OTHERS SO THEY CAN TRUST IN HIM, TOO!

Pray the following prayer right now with all the sincerity you are capable of:

Dear God, You are incredible, holy, and good. I confess that I am a sinner and need You to save me from my sins and the separation it's caused between You and me. I'm sorry for my sins and ask for Your forgiveness.

I believe Jesus Christ died on the cross and rose from the dead so that I can be forgiven, transformed, and have eternal life. I receive Jesus Christ today as my Savior and my Lord so that in His power, I will turn away from sin.

Today I also invite and receive the Holy Spirit to lead my life. I celebrate the promises you've given me for eternal life. I commit to figure out how to put You first in each area of my life, and I will help others know You in all these ways too. Thank You for giving me a new life. I pray this in the name of Jesus, amen.

Too wordy? Want to keep it simple? Say "YES!" to Jesus, being open to whatever that means. That's where it begins. He can change you, daily helping you turn away from sin and any empty attempt to get through life with your own power and perspective.

And if you are here at the end of your reading and have already prayed a prayer like that to launch you into your faith, pause to thank God again for the assurance of His salvation in your life, and then figure out who in the next twenty-four hours you need to share that invitation with so yet another person can become made new in Christ.

HEATHER FLIES

Heather Flies is in her 28th year as the Junior High Pastor at Wooddale Church in Eden Prairie, MN. She LOVES students and people in general! Outside the walls of Wooddale, Heather spends a great deal of time and energy as a communicator, focusing on teenagers. During the school year, she is invited into local schools to speak on abstinence, self-esteem, and relationships. She also encourages women in all seasons of life, trains youth workers, and helps parents understand how to love their teenagers well. Heather loves football, dominating on the tennis court, Tigger, and listening to Christmas music all year long. She owns at least 319 bottles of nail polish and 98 pairs of shorts (which she wears all winter long in Minnesota!). She is the daughter of a long distance truck driver, the youngest of six children, and grew up in southern Minnesota. Heather lives in Minnesota with her husband, Chad, and their two St. Bernards.

ABOUT THE

TONY MYLES

Tony Myles is a multi-faceted ministry veteran, national conference speaker, and author with a passion for the future of the Church. He's served that calling as a Senior Pastor and youth worker, and is a part of the Pastoral Leadership Team at Riverside Church. There, he's a Teaching Pastor and leads the multi-site Student Ministry Team, while also raising up a next generation leadership through internships and residencies. Tony originally grew up in the Chicago area, which made him quite the foodie with a special affection for deep dish pizza and Italian beef sandwiches. Thankfully, he likes exercise, along with traveling to invest into students, church leaders, weekend retreats, college campuses, and more. Mostly, Tony is a "messy Christ-follower" with an overflowing love for God, his bride Katie, his two sons and daughter, and the Church in all its imperfect, redemptive beauty ... and he really likes smoothies.

AUTHORS